LETTERS TO MY GRANDCHILDREN

DAVID

LETTERS TO
MY GRANDCHILDREN

SUZUKI

David Suzuki Foundation

GREYSTONE BOOKS

Vancouver/Berkeley

Thank you, Joane and Tara.
I could not have done what I did without you,
and our children have been my greatest joy.

Greystone Books Ltd.
www.greystonebooks.com

David Suzuki Foundation
219-2211 West 4th Avenue
Vancouver BC Canada V6K 4S2

Cataloguing data available from Library and Archives Canada
ISBN 978-1-77164-088-6 (cloth)
ISBN 978-1-77164-089-3 (epub)

Editing by Nancy Flight
Copy editing by Stephanie Fysh
Jacket design by Jessica Sullivan and Nayeli Jimenez
Text design by Nayeli Jimenez
Jacket photograph by iStockphoto.com
Author photograph by Brendon Purdy
Printed and bound in Canada by Friesens

We gratefully acknowledge the financial support of the Canada Council
for the Arts, the British Columbia Arts Council, the Province of British
Columbia through the Book Publishing Tax Credit, and the Government of
Canada through the Canada Book Fund for our publishing activities.

Greystone Books is committed to reducing the consumption of old-growth
forests in the books it publishes. This book is one step towards that goal.

CONTENTS

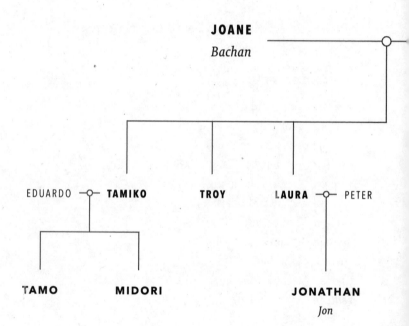

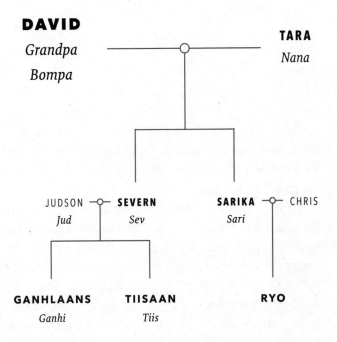

DAVID
Grandpa
Bompa

TARA
Nana

JUDSON — **SEVERN**
Jud — *Sev*

SARIKA — CHRIS
Sari

GANHLAANS
Ganhi

TIISAAN
Tiis

RYO

NOTE TO THE READER

WHEN TAMIKO, MY eldest child, was born, I was overwhelmed with joy at the arrival of another person whom I loved more than my own life. Each of my children has been a wonderful gift who has enriched my life and helped create the person I am today.

I thought fatherhood was the greatest experience of my life—until grandchildren arrived. You see, even in the most wonderful parent–child relationship, there are times when one of us is so pissed off at the other that we scream, fight, pout, or walk off in a huff. Not so with grandchildren. They don't usually live with us, so we don't see each other's faults or have strong disagreements. Grandchildren are pure love; they think we are flawless, and they see us as a constant source of encouragement and support. And when they are young, we feel no guilt about spoiling them (isn't that our job?) and then returning them to Mom and Dad to handle the repercussions.

It took me a while to embrace the notion, but over the past several years I have been introducing myself as an elder. In First Nations societies, elders fill a critical role as the keepers of history, tradition, practical knowledge, and wisdom, and so they are treated with great respect and love. Until recently, under the delusion that I'm still young, I tried to deny that I am an elder. But now I realize that this is the most important period in my life, and in accepting that I'm an elder, I am overwhelmed by the responsibility that this brings. I am obligated to speak the truth now that I am no longer beholden to employers or others who hold some kind of power over me. I have to think about the world that my generation and the boomers who followed are bequeathing to our grandchildren. I am so grateful for the opportunities I've had in my life and I've learned a lot from my mistakes and a few successes, and those lessons should be passed on.

Now that I have entered the last part of my life—what I call the "death zone"—I know that death is inevitable and that I could die at any moment. There is nothing morbid in my thoughts; any elder who doesn't think about death is avoiding some serious issues. And those who think that science is somehow going to "solve" the problem of death or at least stave it off by many more decades are living under a terrible illusion. As a scientist, I know how easy it is to get caught up in the excitement of new discoveries and specu-late about all kinds of wonderful possibilities. Remember Richard Nixon's "war on cancer" or George H.W. Bush's "war on drugs"? Immense amounts of money and effort have been expended to solve these problems, but they are still with us. And I am a biologist, so I understand that aging and death are essential for life and for evolution to occur, especially as conditions are changing so rapidly and require resilience and adaptation. The challenge is not to extend our species' lifespan or to "conquer" death but to ensure that everyone has opportunities to live full and meaningful lives.

Since my grandparents spoke only Japanese and I spoke only English, when I was growing up I was never able to communicate with them beyond superficial greetings and simple exchanges. My mother's parents were so disillusioned with Canada after we lost our rights and were incarcerated during the war that they chose to return to Japan after the war ended. They were on one of the first boats to leave Vancouver and were deposited in the devastation of Hiroshima. Both of my grandparents were dead within a year, so even if I had been able to talk to them as a boy, I wouldn't have had a chance when I was older.

My father's parents chose to stay in Canada after the war and ended up in London, Ontario. The growing extended Suzuki family would gather for dinner at our grandparents' farm on weekends, but, like me, my sisters and cousins couldn't speak Japanese, so we ate at a separate table, where we could chatter away in English. When I had my own family after my grandparents had died, I regretted that I never got to ask them what had motivated them to leave Japan, what it was like when they arrived in Canada, and why they never returned to Japan.

I believe that we learn best by doing, and it has been wonderful to be able to spend time hanging out with my grandchildren. But as I get older, a lot of what I could do in the past—backpacking, skiing, kayaking, even fishing—has become more difficult, and over the years I have reluctantly done these things less often or given them up. More and more, time with my grandchildren has been spent watching, listening, and talking but not doing.

Remembering my unanswered questions for my grandparents, I have often wondered what I would want to say to my grandchildren before I die. I don't want them to have unanswered questions that they wish they had asked. And so the idea of this book was born. I had hoped that writing it would be like talking to them—not a lecture or a straightforward talk, but a kind of loose stream of ideas where one thought might trigger another on a completely different topic and then loop back again. So I began to write as if I was having a conversation—albeit a one-way conversation—with my grandchildren. But their ages extend from twenty-four years to less than a year old, one of the consequences of having two sets of children who range in age from fifty-five to thirty-two.

My original opening line was to be "These words are coming to you from my grave"—the idea being that the book would be written as if I were on my death bed, to be read when all the kids had grown up. But that didn't work because I couldn't imagine what they would each be like as an adult or what the state of the world would be by then, and besides, I'm writing with my full faculties (or at least I think so, though others might disagree). So I've focused on writing about the experiences and thoughts and ideas that I hope my grandchildren will be interested in and will find useful when they have grown up but that will also let them know what made their grandpa tick and why I chose to do what I did. I have left out two big parts of my life—science and the David Suzuki Foundation—which I have covered extensively in two autobiographies.

This book is not a comprehensive overview of my thoughts and priorities—hell, those are sprinkled throughout the books I've already written. These are just some of the things that I hope my grandchildren may find interesting and relevant to their lives. I also hope the book will be read by far more than my own family; I have written it with a current adult audience in mind. And I hope that in reading about my priorities, choices, and motivations, you, the readers, may reflect on your own lives and what matters most for you to pass on.

For you, elders—please step up to the plate. This is the most important time of our lives.

one

IN SEARCH OF ROOTS

MY DARLING GRANDCHILDREN,

I write to you—Tamo, Midori, and Jonathan—as adults, and to you—Ganhi, Tiis, and Ryo—as the older children or young adults you will be when you read this letter. First, though, thank you for sharing your lives with me; it has been a delight to watch each of you since you were a baby and to bear witness to the miracle that every life is. You have been such a joy and have brought so much happiness (and a headache or two) into my life. Thank you, thank you for the privilege of being Grandpa or Bompa to you.

Even though three of you—Tamo, Midori, and Jonathan—were born in the 1990s, you will spend most of your lives in the twenty-first century. And of course, Ganhi, Tiis, and Ryo, your entire lives will be spent in the twenty-first century. The stories from my life that I will recount here will seem like the stuff of history books to you because what is my living memory you know only through books, movies, and videos.

A few years ago, Nana and I visited Japan, and while we were in Yokohama, we visited the last ship (*Hikawa Maru*) to regularly make the trip from Japan to North America. Launched in 1929, it crossed the Pacific from Yokohama to Seattle and carried 75 first-class, 70 tourist-class, and 186 third-class passengers. It's now a museum, and we were fascinated as we walked through it. Each class was on a separate floor and had its own kitchen. First-class passengers travelled in luxury on the top level, with art deco furnishings, lace curtains, and mahogany woodwork. Third-class passengers were confined to the bowels of the hold—deep below the other passengers and next to the immense engines driving the vessel—where it was hot, noisy, and smelly. The royal family had made a trip in that ship, where they occupied the sumptuous top floor. Charlie Chaplin crossed the ocean in the ship as well.

My grandparents had come over much earlier, between 1904 and 1908, and I am sure they travelled in a far less hospitable ship and under worse conditions. They were poor and spent years in Canada paying back the cost of the trip. I imagine they came on a tramp steamer, a cargo ship that took at least three weeks to make the crossing. How tough it must have been, crammed into a tiny space, under heavy seas, with no opportunity to go on deck and breathe fresh air! And remember, there were no television sets, movies, radios, or telephones. Visiting the *Hikawa Maru* filled me with admiration for my grandparents' willingness to take a chance and immigrate to Canada. It must have been a harrowing trip, and they must have felt they were leaving Japan forever.

My father's parents never did make a trip, or even a phone call, back to Japan. After being kept in camps during World War II, my mother's parents decided to leave Canada. They were dropped off in Hiroshima, which had been flattened by the first atomic bomb ever dropped over a city. I can only imagine the suffering of the terribly injured survivors, who had radiation burns and other damage that had never been encountered before, and who needed medical help, food, and shelter. All of Japan had been hammered by war, but Hiroshima was in a category by itself. Not surprisingly, my elderly grandparents both died less than a year after their return.

Why would my grandparents—your great-great-grandparents—leave a country that was their home for an unknown future in Canada? Like desperate people today fleeing Vietnam, Haiti, or Cuba and crossing treacherous bodies of water to get to new lands, my father's parents were driven by poverty so severe that it was worth it to them to take that risk.

Japan was in the throes of shedding its feudal class system of shoguns, samurai, farmers, craftspeople, and merchants to follow a Western industrial path. Grandpa Suzuki apprenticed as a carpenter when he was a teenager and became a superb boatbuilder in Canada. Suzuki boats had an excellent reputation, and I hear there is a Suzuki-built boat still in use on Vancouver Island. Grandpa Nakamura was a disenfranchised samurai—a member of Japan's warrior aristocracy—and never did hold down a job. Grandma Nakamura was a nurse, and she was revered for treating people during the horrendous epidemic of Spanish flu in 1918. My mother's most important hope was to be reunited with her mother after she died.

When my grandparents arrived in Vancouver, it was a resource town built on mining, fishing, and logging and drew people from all over the world. It was a rough-and-tumble place, where racist assumptions about people of colour were embedded in the culture. After all, when Europeans first arrived in North America, they claimed to have "discovered" it, despite the hundreds of thousands of people living in rich and varied cultures all across the continent. Because the indigenous people were completely alien to the incoming Europeans, they were dismissed as "primitive."

The newcomers were focused on finding wealth and had little interest in the indigenous people, flora, and fauna except as resources. They regarded indigenous people as savages who were impediments to exploitation and so should be eliminated or be forced to adopt European ways. This attitude continued through the twentieth century, when indigenous children were sent to residential schools and their languages and traditional ways were officially banned. Asians and blacks, too, were considered different and assumed to be inferior and so were not given the right to vote or, in many parts of the province of British Columbia, to own property. They were also prohibited from entering certain professions, such as medicine and pharmacy. That was British Columbia and much of Canada in the early twentieth century.

Each of you is a quarter Japanese, so I hope you find your Asian heritage of interest. My knowledge of Japanese history is pretty minimal, but I have been intrigued by the way the country was brought into the global community. For over two and a half centuries (1603–1868), Japan had deliberately isolated itself from the rest of the world, rebuffing attempts to open its ports for foreign traffic and trade. This was called the Edo, or Tokugawa, period, when Japan was under the rule of the Tokugawa family. The ruling class was kept in power by the samurai class, trained fighters who made up about 5 percent of the population. Below the samurai was the peasant class, 80 percent of the people. As in every civilization throughout time, it was these people who grew food who enabled other kinds of activities to evolve. Below the peasants were the craftspeople, and below them were the merchants, who sold what the craftspeople made. There was also a class called Eta, or *burakumin,* who were referred to as "untouchables." They were considered contaminated because they disposed of dead people, butchered animals, or worked with animal skins. In modern Japan, class distinctions are supposed to be gone, but *burakumin* still suffer tremendous discrimination.

Under the Tokugawas, Japanese culture flourished and the economy grew during a long period of relative peace and isolation. Today we hear over and over how globalization of economies is critical to our future prosperity, but the history of the Edo period offers a different lesson. (And for the past twenty years, Japan's economy has been flat. We keep hearing that a failure to keep the economy growing will be a disaster, but Japan disproves that notion.)

In 1853, U.S. commodore Matthew Perry and four heavily armed "black ships" steamed into Edo (Tokyo) Bay, demonstrating the advanced military technology of steamships and cannons and demanding access to Japanese harbours. The following year a treaty was signed that ended Japan's isolation from the rest of the world and prepared the way for the 1868 Meiji Restoration, under Emperor Meiji, a period that combined Western technological advances with traditional Eastern values. Iron smelters, shipyards, and spinning mills sprang up as Japan became industrialized and built up its military power. The samurai no longer had a position as a class in a nation on the way to Western-style industrial development.

The rapid change made by the Japanese after Perry shows that dramatic social and economic transformation is possible in a short time. In the 1930s Japan veered into militarism and ended up in a world war that it lost in 1945. But again, forced by military defeat and devastation of the country, Japan rose from that terrible time to become an economic giant within a few decades. Today we are told that changing from fossil fuels to renewable energy will not only destroy the economy but also throw us back into the Dark Ages. I don't believe it. If we can pull together as a society, as Japan has done, all kinds of changes are possible.

And thanks to Commodore Perry, you are all here. Grandpa Nakamura was born at a time when there was no longer a place for him as a samurai, and the end of Japan's global isolation meant all of my grandparents had the chance to move to Canada.

NANA AND I had an opportunity to find out more about Grandpa Nakamura when she and I were in Japan taking care of you, Ganhi and Tiis, while your mom and dad were on a speaking tour there. Did you two know that your mom is like a rock star in Japan?

In 1992, when she was twelve, she attended the Earth Summit in Rio and gave a speech that became famous and has been published in textbooks in Japan. As a result, she is well known among young people there. I think the fact that she looks Asian and has a part-Japanese last name (Cullis-Suzuki) means Japanese kids can identify with her.

One of the places where she spoke on her tour was Kyushu, south of Honshu, the big island where Tokyo and Kyoto are located. I knew that Grandpa Nakamura was from Kumamoto, on Kyushu, so we decided to see whether we could find out anything about him. Sure enough, we discovered that he had been trained as a samurai and that he had gone to a very elite high school, which we visited. There we learned that he had been unable to carry on as a samurai and had applied to enter the navy but was rejected because of bad eyesight. Perhaps that was the reason he decided to come to Canada.

I don't think he ever worked in Canada. Since he was born into nobility, working was not part of his background. There is one story about him that I love but that may not be true. He was in Trail, a mining town in British Columbia, when the workers at one of the mines went on strike. The company decided to break the strike by bringing in "scabs"—people who were willing to do the work for low wages—and many happened to be Japanese. The strikers threatened to beat up any scab who tried to cross the picket line, and the Japanese were terrified. They asked Grandpa Nakamura to lead them past the strikers, and he agreed. When he walked up to the strikers, they could tell by the way he carried himself that he was tough, so they moved aside and let the men in. Great story, even if it is about strikebreaking—which I don't support.

My grandparents never learned to speak more than a primitive level of English. They knew Japanese people in Canada who spoke English well enough to help them get established, and as their kids—my parents—grew up, they interpreted for their parents. I never learned to speak Japanese, because after the war, Mom and Dad were anxious that we be Canadians and not draw attention to our differences by speaking another language.

How I regret that! The more languages we know, the richer our lives can be. I studied French for five years, Latin for four years, and German for three years, all in high school.

But I have needed Spanish for the many Latin American countries I've done work in. Tamo and Midori, you are so fortunate that your dad took you to Chile and other coun- 9 tries in South America and that you learned Spanish.

I never got to ask my grandparents why they left Japan, what the trip was like, what the conditions were when they arrived, and whether they were glad they had come. So many questions that will never be answered! I never got a chance to thank them for making that incredible journey and enduring the hardships in this foreign place so that their children would have a better future and their grandchildren—my sisters and I—could grow up as Canadians.

My grandparents are called issei, the first generation of Japanese in Canada. My parents, your great-grandparents, were born in Vancouver—Dad in 1909 and Mom in 1911—and are called nisei (second generation, but first Canadian-born). They were among the first nisei in Canada and truly straddled the two cultures, being fluently bilingual in Japanese and English. Their knowledge of Japan was only second-hand, however, as neither ever lived in Japan (Dad went for a month when he was five). Because they were bilingual, they carried out all the family transactions in English from an early age, and their parents felt less and less pressure to learn the language. And because my parents had to work when they were still young and act as interpreters for their parents in everything they did, Mom and Dad both grew up fast.

I am a sansei (third generation), and like most of those in my generation, I was born around the time of World War II, when Japan was the enemy, and so I was not encouraged to speak Japanese. During the war my grandparents must have been torn emotionally—they had relatives in Japan, but they had moved to Canada.

Each subsequent generation is also identified by the number of generations since the first generation of Japanese arrived here. Your moms, my daughters, are yonsei (fourth generation). You are all gosei (fifth generation), but by now your Japanese heritage is pretty diluted. Ganhi and Tiis, you are half Haida, so it's ridiculous to consider you fifth-generation Japanese, especially when your dad's ancestry in Canada goes back perhaps thousands of years.

My mother and father, like most nisei at that time, grew up without elders or grandparents because those generations remained in Japan. My parents' primary connection to the "old country" was through language, food, and some cultural activities, like *odori* (dance) or martial arts such as judo or kendo.

Can you imagine growing up without ever knowing Bachan (my first wife and grandmother to three of you), Nana, or me? Until recently, this lack of grandparents and other elders was significant for children of immigrants to all new and distant lands, not just Canada, because it meant they had only the shallowest of roots to the old country and no roots at all in the new one. Today, of course, we have long-distance phone calls, Skype, and jet travel to keep us connected with elders who live far away.

ALTHOUGH THE ISSEI who arrived here at the beginning
of the twentieth century faced anti-Asian racism and discrimination, Canada offered opportunities that Japan didn't.
When the issei arrived, they did not have the historical or
cultural attachment to the land that indigenous people have,
and so they saw it as a commodity or real estate. If there
were fish, catch them and sell them; if there were trees, cut
them down and sell them; if there were minerals, dig them
up and sell them; if there was rich soil, plant vegetables and
sell them. Everything was a resource to exploit for economic
return. That's why people sought new lands, and that's the
way it's been with new immigrants ever since the great wave
of exploration, conquest, and settlement in North and South
America, Africa, Australia, and New Zealand that began more
than five centuries ago.

As you know, Nana and I have worked a lot with First
Nations people in Canada and with other indigenous communities in other parts of the world. We have learned so
much from them about radically different ways of seeing
the land. For people who have lived in an area for thousands
of years rather than decades or even centuries, land is far
more than a commodity; it is their home and is sacred.

Indigenous people didn't automatically venerate the
earth, however. They learned to respect it through the
mistakes and insights of their ancestors. Remember, my
background is in genetics, and I have been amazed to see
how scientists can use DNA, our genetic material, to trace

the movement of people across the planet over time. And all trails lead back to Africa 150,000 years ago. That's the birthplace of our species, meaning that we are all Africans by origin.

Can you imagine what Africa must have been like when humans first appeared on the planet? The plains must have been teeming with animals in abundance and variety far beyond anything we would see in the Serengeti today. And if we think about our earliest ancestors, who would have been a small group of people lacking in size, speed, and strength, as well as acuity of vision, hearing, and smell, compared with the other creatures, we have to wonder how we ever survived with all the large, strong, fleet-footed animals around. Our big advantage was the two-kilogram organ buried deep in our skulls—the human brain. It endowed us with a prodigious memory, insatiable curiosity, keen observation, and astonishing creativity, qualities that compensated for our inferior physical and sensory abilities.

The Nobel Prize–winning French geneticist François Jacob once told me that the human brain has an "inbuilt need for order." In other words, we don't like it when things happen that don't make sense to us. So, as curious creatures, constantly looking, tinkering, and learning, we acquired knowledge about our surroundings, and, if Jacob is right (and I think he is), we had an itch to put everything together in a cohesive picture of interconnection and causal relationships, or what some call a worldview, in which everything is connected and nothing exists separate and in isolation.

Using their big brains, early humans found ways to exploit their surroundings. They could coat themselves in mud or camouflage themselves with grass or branches to sneak up on prey. They could dig pits to trap animals, spear even bigger creatures like mammoths, drive animals over cliffs along walls of rocks they had placed there. With simple baskets or wooden hooks, they caught fish. They made shelters in caves using rocks, branches, and reeds. What observant, imaginative animals our ancestors were! They had to be to survive.

As their numbers increased, things they found uses for—certain trees, medicinal plants, mammals, and birds—would have decreased in number, and there would be pressure to find more resources (and maybe teenagers wanted to find some excitement and check out the Neanderthal ladies over the mountain, since there is evidence that humans and Neanderthals crossbred). In their search for more resources, people began to explore beyond their normal territory. As they moved into new territories, they found more big, slow-moving animals that were easy targets. What I find amazing is that even with such simple tools as spears, clubs, and stone axes, those early people were able to drive species to extinction.

Scientists suggest that humans eliminated mammoths (one animal would have fed a lot of people for quite a while), giant elk, marsupial lions, giant sloths, and aurochs. As humans moved into new areas, they extirpated some of the plants and animals. When people reached Australia over forty thousand years ago, the continent was covered with a vast forest. Those early migrants brought the technology of fire, and burning remains a key part of Australian aboriginal culture today. As a result, the entire country has been completely transformed.

Tamo, Midori, and Jonathan, you may have heard the classic story about Easter Island. When Europeans arrived there, they found giant stone carvings of heads. But people lived lives of extreme poverty and violence, often raiding and even eating each other. How could such miserable people have had the knowledge and ability to carve the monoliths? Then the Europeans found the place where the stone was quarried and discovered that the stones had been moved to the sites along the island's edges on rollers made of trees. The island had once been covered in forest, and at some point, the people must have seen that it was disappearing as it was being overcut. Yet they continued cutting until all the trees were gone, and their way of life disappeared. At least that's one way people have constructed the story.

Early people learned through their mistakes that their survival and well-being were utterly dependent on nature. They also came to understand that we are created by Earth's fundamental elements—earth, air, fire, and water—and therefore that Earth is our mother.

Over very long periods of time, as people moved to different parts of Earth, they began to recognize that nature was the source of their lives and livelihood and that Earth should be treated with respect and care. This knowledge became the basis of indigenous understanding and cultures, which are the result of hard-earned lessons gained over thousands of years. That is why it is so important to fight to keep those cultures alive. Once they are gone, they will never be reproduced.

This is not to say that indigenous people are always in balance with nature. But they have a different perspective on our relationship with our surroundings. Thinking of the biosphere as Mother Earth and understanding that we are literally created by her body of air, water, earth, and sunlight is radically different from thinking of the world as a resource; when that happens, Mother Earth becomes a motherlode. And indigenous people have learned this truth by their own acts of extinguishing plants and animals.

I HAVE TOLD you these stories because they have been an important part of my learning, and I hope they will help you understand your place in the world. Ganhi and Tiis, your Haida father and *nannai* (grandmother) and *chinnai* (grandfather) have taught Nana and me a great deal and have already instilled in you that sense of connectedness to place. Tamo, Midori, Jonathan, and Ryo, I hope you have also gained that sense from us.

two

RACISM

MY DEAREST GRANDCHILDREN,

You are growing up in a very different time from when I was a boy. Even though I was a Canadian, born in Canada like my mom and dad, we were suspect because we were of Japanese descent. Equality before the law, freedom of speech and movement, and the right to vote are principles of democracy that you all take for granted, but they did not always apply to everyone. Ganhi and Tiisaan, you know your *nannai*'s and *chinnai*'s parents couldn't vote because they were Haida, and my parents couldn't either. It's important to remember that and to understand that today you might not feel discriminated against, but that bigots who hate Muslims, Jews, gays, or any other group because of colour, religion, ethnic group, sexual orientation, or even poverty could just as easily turn against you because they are ignorant and, in their

16

ignorance, are afraid of people who look different or behave differently. We must always stick up for someone who is being picked on because one day it could be our turn, as it already has been. 17

It's funny how when we are kids, we don't see the differences that adults do. We learn what to fear or hate from our parents or others around us. When I was a boy and we were living in the small town of Leamington, Ontario, a friend and I were playing in an empty lot one day when Dad came by from work on his bike. I yelled to him and he waved back. My friend looked at me wide-eyed. "How do you know him?" he asked.

I laughed and said, "He's my dad, dummy!"

"But he's a chink!" my friend blurted out.

I didn't know whether to laugh or to be mad because he had used a racial slur. But I realized that when we played together colour made no difference. Yet he could see racial differences, as he recognized in Dad, and he must have been told something bad about "chinks." Nana has said that when she was growing up in West Vancouver, she only knew of one family of Chinese people at her school. Yet when it was pointed out that one of her teachers was Chinese, she said, "I didn't think of him as Chinese; he was just my math teacher."

We're all aware of differences in people, and these differences can run in families. I remember a girl whose red hair was just like her dad's, and, Ganhi, your dimple is exactly like Nana's. These are examples of "traits" or "characteristics" that seem to be passed on from one generation to the next.

You know that as a scientist I studied heredity. In very early times, tens of thousands of years ago, when people lived as nomadic tribal folk, they may have been able to recognize similar physical traits in people from their territory and must have known about similarities that ran in families. But when the Agricultural Revolution occurred about ten thousand years ago, and people realized that seeds could be collected and planted to produce plants that could be eaten or used for some other purpose, farmers began to apply the basic concept that defines genetics: like begets like. That means if you breed the offspring of, say, sheep that have slightly longer hair or plants that grow bigger fruit, chances are they will give rise to longer hair or bigger fruit. That is still a basic principle of genetics today. What is remarkable is that within a few thousand years, those early farmers were able to select most strains of animals and plants in forms that we would recognize today.

Domestication of plants and animals transformed our way of living. Because people were able to settle down instead of following animals and plants through the seasons, they could now rely on a stable source of food. Settled in one place, people could build permanent homes and villages. And because people now lived together in one place, agriculture ultimately gave rise to complex civilization and cities.

But the misunderstanding of heredity plagues us to this day. In the late nineteenth and early twentieth centuries, people believed that differences in class, wealth, and gender roles were inherited biologically. So an aristocrat or a nobleman would feel justified in considering all of his privileges a "birthright," sanctioned not only by the law but also by biology. In the same way, the idea that a "woman's place was in the home" was defended as a reflection of biological difference.

Modern genetics began as a discipline in 1900, when rules governing heredity that had been defined earlier by a monk named Gregor Mendel were rediscovered. The field exploded as scientists working on heredity in plants and animals made spectacular discoveries that genes are located on chromosomes, that radiation and chemicals induce mutations, that genes determine the production of proteins in the body, and so on. Not surprisingly, but insidiously, scientists began to apply findings from their new field to human behaviour and intelligence. Now scientists began to say that there was a hereditary basis for intellectual differences, criminality, laziness, drunkenness. A whole field arose, called eugenics, which looked at how to improve the hereditary qualities of people and which attracted some of the top scientists of the day. Eugenics courses were taught in universities, and eugenics journals and professional societies were established. At fairs, eugenics booths displayed posters purporting to show through family trees that criminality, poverty, and mental defects were inherited traits, and calling for people with such defects to be sterilized. Not surprisingly, those qualities seen to be desirable and therefore encouraged to be passed on were sobriety, church attendance, diligence, and being educated, traits exhibited by white and upper-middle-class people.

20   Laws were passed in North America in response to many of these ideas. Eugenics acts allowed the sterilization of patients in mental institutions to prevent further inheritance of "bad" genes. And in Canada, especially the province of Alberta, those laws were enforced until the mid-twentieth century. In the United States, acts were passed to restrict immigration of people from countries considered "inferior" or "undesirable," traits that were assumed to be not cultural or social but hereditary. Several states passed laws preventing intermarriage between two people of different racial backgrounds on the assumption that mixing of genes would lead to "disharmonious combinations." Under such laws, that would have meant that Nana and I and all of your parents would not have been able to marry and none of you would ever have been born! What is ironic is that hybrid corn is the basis of a lot of farming today, a result of the observation that two different highly inbred strains of corn (like different racial or ethnic groups), when interbred, lead to "hybrid vigour," or "heterosis," which means that the offspring are much more vigorous in size, health, and survival than either parental strain. And I feel that is true when I see many "hapas," or offspring of interracial couples.

I've always been keen to inform people and raise the alarm about the misapplication of the rules of heredity. When the Nazis and Hitler came into prominence in the 1930s, Germany was a power in science and culture in Europe. Using genetics as the rationale, the Nazis enacted racial purification laws, according to which gypsies, Jews, and mentally unstable people were sterilized and ultimately exterminated in death camps. When the camps were liberated at the end of the war and the terrible slaughter, especially of Jews, was revealed, people reacted with revulsion to the grotesque consequences of extrapolating far beyond solid data. Although no new genetic insights had been gained, scientists reversed themselves and proclaimed that most of the traits deemed by eugenics to have been hereditary were shaped by the environment, not heredity.

You may think this is all academic stuff that happened a long time ago, but it directly affected me and Nannai and Chinnai. The whole history of treatment of the First Nations, who had rich, diverse cultures and occupied all of Canada at the time of contact with Europeans, is based on racism— their assumed inferiority and backwardness. By imposing a completely alien system of treaties in a foreign language on the First Nations, British and French people took their lands, and promises made in those treaties were not lived up to by the colonizers. The whole thrust of the new government was to break the connection with the land and to inculcate the First Nations with British or French values. This process is shockingly described in Tom King's book *The Inconvenient Indian*. The consequences of this policy to stamp out indigenous beliefs and values can be seen in every First Nations community in North America, as well as in the state of indigenous peoples in Australia, New Zealand, South America, and Africa.

These assumptions about heredity and race had a direct effect on me when Canada imposed the War Measures Act in 1942. Because Japan had launched a "sneak attack" on Pearl Harbor, on December 7, 1941, it was widely believed that "treachery" was a racial trait of Japanese people, and even though we were Canadians, my family could not be trusted. All our rights of citizenship were suspended. Bank accounts were frozen. And eventually, we ended up in the British Columbia interior in a town at the foot of mountains that are now part of Valhalla Provincial Park.

I was six when we took that long train trip from Vancouver. For me as a kid, it was a grand adventure and I wasn't aware that all the other passengers on the train were Japanese. What chokes me up is knowing that my parents were just in their early thirties, and their world, their hopes, and their dreams were dashed when they were suddenly considered enemy aliens of their birth country. From then on, they were subject to decisions made by politicians and bureaucrats in the nation's capital of Ottawa or the provincial capital of Victoria and were helpless to do anything about it.

My father had volunteered to go to a road camp near Revelstoke, where they were building the trans-Canada highway. He thought that by volunteering, he would indicate his good intentions and save his family from being sent away to camps. But he was mistaken. While he was in a camp taking care of the horses used for logging, we, his family, were being held in the remote Slocan Valley.

A story that I can't tell without crying is about the time Dad was injured by a log that rolled over his leg. Because of the injury, he got a pass from the camp doctor to leave camp. Now remember, he was born and raised in Canada and had only been to Japan for a month when he was a boy, but he was a prisoner. Armed with a piece of paper enabling him to leave camp (the doctor assumed he wanted to go to a nearby village), he took a bus to Nakusp, a town where he could get a ferry across Upper Arrow Lake to Slocan City, where we were staying. It was called a city because it had boomed during the silver rush of the 1890s, but when the rush was over, it became a derelict village of decaying buildings. Dad didn't want to attract attention to himself in Nakusp and get caught, so he found a hotel to stay in but didn't go out to eat. In the morning he boarded a ferry.

By the time the ferry started, he hadn't eaten for a day and was very hungry. He smelled food on the boat and found a kitchen, where he spotted a Chinese cook. In the 1930s, Japan had invaded Manchuria and China, and the bitter enmity between the Japanese and the Chinese had carried over to Canada. Dad's heart sank when the cook saw him and called out to him to come in. Dad was sure the man was going to sound the alarm and report him. "You're Japanese, aren't you?" the cook asked, and Dad nodded. "Sit down and eat," the cook said. "We're all brothers." He served Dad a big meal and handed him a sandwich to take with him after he had eaten—no charge. That act of kindness was courageous as well as generous, and I will be ever grateful to that man, who saw through the racial hatred and treated my father as a fellow human being.

When Dad got to Slocan, he had no idea where we were living, but he knew that there was still no school and that my sisters and I would probably be somewhere near a playground. He could hear children playing, and sure enough, Auntie Marcia, Auntie Aiko, and I were there. Dad called out to us, but because he had been working outside for several months, he was heavily tanned and had lost a lot of weight. I didn't recognize him. But Marcia recognized his voice and immediately ran to him. Dad always got emotional when he talked about the moment we ran into his arms.

Mom was delighted to see Dad, of course, but she was working as a secretary for the Royal Canadian Mounted Police—the Mounties—and was afraid they would catch him. So the next day at work, she confided to one of the officers that Dad had taken a big risk to visit her and asked what he should do. The officer said he wouldn't tell anyone but that Dad should skedaddle back to the camp. So two days after arriving, Dad left to go back to the road camp. A few months later he was allowed to return to Slocan and stay with us. My sister Dawn was born nine months after his first visit.

In the camp, most of the kids were nisei and were fluently bilingual. I couldn't speak any Japanese, so they picked on me. Many of their parents were angry at what the government had done to them and must have talked about hoping that Japan would give Canada a drubbing. I was so clueless that I didn't understand why we were in the camp or even that there was a war going on. To my parents' credit, somehow they shielded us from their anger and fears and difficulties. But for the first time, I experienced bigotry—in the way other Japanese Canadian kids treated me, because I only spoke English. I felt like an outcast in the village and preferred to stay away from the other kids. But it was a fantastic place to be a child who didn't have a school to go to. I spent hours and hours wandering around the lake, fishing in the creek, and hiking up the mountains. Remember, we had no telephones or radio, and television had yet to be invented.

You all know my dad was an avid fisherman, and one of his pride and joys was a revolutionary reel he had bought before the war—a spinning reel. Most people had never seen one before. Dad had taken it to the road camp and then brought it with him to Slocan. We were forbidden to fish or have a camera, but Dad fished and also had a camera (I have no idea how he got film or had it developed). In early spring, whitefish would come close to the shore in huge numbers to spawn. They would blacken the bottom of the lake, occasionally flashing silver as they turned on their sides. Whitefish are wonderful eating, with a firm, pale flesh, and Dad had an idea for catching the fish—he would put a treble hook on the line, and a white rag on the hook so that he could see it and snag the fish. His idea worked like a charm because there were so many fish.

Once I was posted as a lookout for the Mounties as Dad and a friend hauled in fish after fish, but I got so carried away by the action that I forgot to watch out. Someone reported us (Dad thinks it was a jealous Japanese person), and a Mountie came right up from behind and nabbed us. As he walked us back to our apartment, he admired Dad's spinning reel. "Pretty nice outfit," he mused. "I've never seen one of those. You know, it would be a shame for me to confiscate it. Why don't you tie a hook on a line and wrap it around a stick and I'll turn *that* in." It was an incredible act of generosity on the officer's part and helped ease a lot of my pain at failing to do my job. Because of that act of humanity, I've always had a soft spot for the RCMP.

So it pains me, Tamo, to see the way you were treated by them when they arrested you for protesting the Kinder Morgan pipeline at Burnaby Mountain, especially since they deliberately pulled you across the line in order to seize you. And then you were harassed by another Mountie, who accused you of deliberately jumping across the line and attacking the officer—it was such a trumped-up story, it took my breath away. I am disappointed that the RCMP doesn't understand that its high standing has to be earned. It seems that every time there's an accusation of wrongdoing on the part of government, police, or corporations like pharmaceutical, fossil fuel, chemical, agro-, or forestry companies, the initial response is always denial rather than an immediate concern that they might be real and a commitment to get to the truth.

But to get back to the war years... As you might expect in a country at war, food was scarce. As a group suspected of having connections with the enemy, and having been sent to a remote part of the province, we did not receive great food. Rice was constantly in short supply, and I believe Dad's prowess at fishing made an important contribution to our diet. But this remote valley had also attracted Doukhobors, Russians who had been persecuted for their religious beliefs and had fled to Canada to live and worship as they wished. They had chosen this remote place so that they would be left alone. They were superb farmers, and I remember Doukhobor men visiting us in their horse-drawn wagons laden with fresh vegetables—a welcome addition to our diet, though I have no idea how my parents raised the money to buy them. But I think the Doukhobors empathized with us because of how badly we were treated, and I've always been grateful to them for their role in feeding us.

The main job of parents is to shield their children from the difficulties and realities of the adult world, and in that, Mom and Dad succeeded amazingly. We felt loved and protected, and the environment around us was a constant source of wonder and joy. We didn't know that as the war was coming to an end, British Columbia sensed an opportunity to get rid of one of its "yellow peril" threats. The province urged the federal government to offer us two choices: sign an agreement to give up Canadian citizenship for a one-way trip to Japan—a foreign country to my parents, my sisters, and me—or leave British Columbia and move east of the Rockies. As you might imagine, people in the camps were pissed off at how we had been treated, and many decided to express their anger by signing up to go to Japan. In fact, some leaders of this movement urged people to sign up and intimidated those who didn't. Dad wanted desperately to stay in British Columbia, but that didn't seem to be an option. One night he came home looking very sad and told my mother that he thought we should go to Japan. I yelled that I didn't want to go. We couldn't speak Japanese, and we were Canadians. I threw myself on the bed crying hysterically. It wasn't an act; I did not want to go. Perhaps Dad was just testing us, but the next day, he said we would stay in Canada. I learned much later that my parents had been branded *inu* (dogs) and shunned, as more than 90 percent of people were convinced or coerced into signing to "repatriate" (though most would be going for the first time, not repatriating).

Those signing on to stay in Canada were soon sent to staging sites in preparation for being moved out east. My family was sent to Kaslo, in the Kootenays.

The tight communities from Japantown in Vancouver and from the fishing village of Steveston were broken up by the evacuation and postwar dispersal of Japanese Canadians, who showed their resilience and resourcefulness in settling in communities across Canada. The economic recovery and success of the Japanese Canadians, their high academic performance, and their assimilation as seen in a high rate of intermarriage are often cited as a positive consequence of the evacuation and dispersal, but ends never justify the means. For me, the history of how Canada treated Japanese Canadians during World War II forces us to ask, what is this country, and what does it mean to be a citizen?

ON APRIL 4, 1968, the great U.S. civil rights leader Martin Luther King was assassinated. In the agony that followed his death, students at the University of British Columbia organized an outdoor gathering in his memory and asked me to speak. I talked about how fortunate the civil rights movement had been to have such a powerful leader as King and promised that the struggle would continue. Then I said that King's death should not make us feel smug but should remind Canadians of our own history of racism, from our treatment of the original peoples to the Japanese Canadian evacuation and incarceration. An editorial in one of the local newspapers chastised me for bringing up the Japanese experience when it had nothing to do with the kind of racism that had led to King's assassination.

I also received a letter from a woman from a prominent BC family telling me that the threat from Japan during World War II had been very real and that the government had had to act to reduce the danger. I wrote back that although she looked at me and saw a Japanese person, I and my family were all Canadians, born and raised here, so Japan had been my enemy too. It was racist to assume that because I was genetically identical to Japanese people in Japan, I too should be treated as the enemy.

After the war, Japan rose like a phoenix to become an economic powerhouse, and names like Sony, Toyota, and Canon became familiar around the world as icons of the country's enormous industrial creativity. As a result, I found that being Japanese no longer elicited the kind of prejudice we had lived with before and during the war. But bigotry still exists, and it reflects closed minds, ignorance, and fear of difference. If we witness an act of discrimination but do not speak up or intervene, then we tacitly support it.

I once met a Chinese Canadian woman who lives in a Vancouver neighbourhood where there is a pocket of First Nations people. This woman, who had herself experienced bigotry against Chinese, described Native people in a stereotypical way, which I challenged. To my surprise, instead of admitting it might be bigoted to characterize all Native people the same way, she continued to justify her opinions on the basis of her personal encounters with First Nations individuals. When those who are victims of discrimination become bigots themselves, then bigotry triumphs.

I hope that all of you will speak out against racism and other forms of bigotry whenever you encounter it.

three

FORGOTTEN LESSONS FROM THE GREAT DEPRESSION

MY LOVELY ONES,

Another evil to be fought against is greed. Tamo, Midori, and Jonathan, do you remember the financial crisis of 2008? Your parents probably shielded you from it. Banks and other financial institutions nearly collapsed, the stock market took a nosedive, and many people lost their homes or their savings. The only reason we weren't plunged into a stock market crash and a full-blown depression was that U.S. president Barack Obama injected hundreds of billions of dollars into the teetering banks that had created the crisis, to keep them afloat. A full-blown depression would have caused unimaginable suffering around the world, but we in the rich countries would have had it the worst because so few of us have any idea how to be self-sufficient. It would have been a huge comeuppance for societies like ours, which live as if we can and must grow forever in order to serve our constant demand for more stuff. We would have received a much-needed lesson in humility and would have had to reassess what life is all about.

A major depression did occur during the lives of your great-grandparents, my parents. In 1929, people were trying to get rich quick, not by producing innovative products, but by speculating on the stock market. Just as miners in the nineteenth century hoped to get rich by striking gold, people in the 1920s hoped they could get rich by buying stock that they thought would suddenly shoot up in price. The result was an inflated market, but no real value was added to the economy. When people began to fear that the banks might shut down, they panicked and pulled their money out, triggering the crash that led to the Great Depression. I am sure it was far more complex than this, but this is my layperson's simplified history. The Great Depression of the 1930s lasted for years and was a painful time. Stories abound of people who had made millions suddenly becoming paupers and jumping out of windows. People "rode the rails," hitching rides on trains to search for jobs. I remember Dad telling me how he travelled from town to town in British Columbia on top of trains and how people died of suffocation from coal smoke as the trains wound through long tunnels. He would stop in "hobo jungles" where one could find pots and pans and people to share meals, and farmers would grow extra rows of vegetables so that people passing through could feed themselves before moving on in search of work.

Back then there were no social safety nets, such as welfare or unemployment insurance or government-funded health care. There were "soup kitchens," where people could get food, but most people struggled to get by. Family and community were absolutely necessary to survive those times. During that terrible crucible of suffering, my parents became adults, got married, and had a family. You can imagine the kind of lessons that the experience of this time etched into their lives and that then were passed on to us, their children.

They counselled us to live within our means and to use our money sparingly for the "necessities" in life. Conspicuous consumption was frowned on as showing off. What pulled the country out of the Depression was World War II, which provided jobs not just for soldiers but for those producing weapons and war machines. But what would keep the economy going when peace returned and the production of armaments would no longer be necessary? That's what U.S. president Franklin Delano Roosevelt asked the Council of Economic Advisers to the President. Its solution was consumption.

This notion was expressed by retailing analyst Victor Lebow: "Our enormously productive economy... demands that we make consumption our way of life, that we convert the buying and use of goods into rituals, that we seek our spiritual satisfaction, our ego satisfaction, in consumption... We need things consumed, burned up, worn out, replaced and discarded at an ever accelerating rate."[1]

In 1959, the chairman of President Eisenhower's Council of Economic Advisers stated that the American economy's "ultimate purpose" was "to produce more consumer goods," which now seems to be assumed as a fundamental part of economies. According to Pablo Ruiz Nápoles, a Mexican academic, "For contemporary economic theory, in general, consumption, the satisfaction of human needs, is the final aim of economic activity."[2]

The idea was to keep the economy growing by offering more and more stuff for people to buy. But if something is made well, then eventually the market will be saturated. There are ways to keep it growing anyway: making sure that fashions keep changing; seeking new consumers, such as younger and younger people, poorer people, and people in developing countries; bringing out new models of things, with slightly different shapes and more bells and whistles; setting "best before" dates on consumable items. Still, if the primary role of the consumer item is filled, the market will decrease.

Disposable products ensure a never-ending market but come at a cost to Earth. It is the hyperconsumption driven by the need of industrialized countries to keep their economies growing that is the primary cause of ecological devastation today.

After the tragedy of 9/11, President George W. Bush asked Americans, on September 20, 2001, for "continued participation and confidence in the American economy." Reporting on the speech for *Time* magazine, Frank Pellegrini added, "And for God's sake, keep shopping."[3]

As our political leaders rush to embrace the benefits of a global economy, they forfeit any hope of controlling or managing the economy nationally. When Brian Mulroney was prime minister of Canada and appeared on *Larry King Live* on CNN, King suggested that Canada's economy wasn't very strong. Mulroney replied that he couldn't be blamed for what happened in the global economy, which was beyond his control. Exactly, but then why embrace it?

I'm not an economist, but in 1933, one of the giants of economics, John Maynard Keynes, wrote, "I sympathize... with those who would minimize, rather than those who would maximize, economic entanglement between nations. Ideas, knowledge, art, hospitality, travel—these are the things which should of their nature be international. But let goods be homespun whenever it is reasonably and conveniently possible, and, above all, let finance be primarily national."[4]

Globalization provides countries with access to a larger market for a nation's goods and thus can add to corporate opportunities, but in a time when brand names like Coca-Cola, McDonald's, Toyota, and Nike determine our choices, globalization hides local ecological and social consequences. We buy a brand unaware of the health and ecological costs of growing cotton, mining metals, depleting resources, or polluting waters. We just want the brand product, so we pay the money and use it. But the act of buying has repercussions that reverberate invisibly around the globe.

After World War II, when we left British Columbia to move to Ontario, we were destitute, though as kids we never saw ourselves as "poor." But because of my parents' experience during the Depression, all through my childhood we were exhorted with slogans such as "You don't get anything for nothing" and "There is no such thing as a free lunch." The most important of these mini-lessons was that we had to work hard. We were expected to go to work, and I don't ever remember my sisters or me complaining that we were too tired or didn't want to work. There was no point, because we all had to.

In Ontario in 1946, I was ten years old, and that was the first summer I worked for money. We would do "piecework" (meaning that we'd get paid by the amount of work we did) on farms, and the first job I remember was picking strawberries and raspberries—for a nickel or dime a basket, depending on the size of the basket. My mother was a whiz at picking, and no matter how fast I picked, she always beat me handily. All the money we earned went to Mom. There was no such thing as an allowance for us; we contributed to the family, and in return, our parents took care of our food, clothing, and school things. One of the problems with that is that I wore what clothes I had, usually blue jeans and a work shirt. I never paid attention to style or fashion because my folks bought my clothes. So I have no fashion sense and I don't care.

We worked on different crops through the growing season. I loved picking tomatoes because of the incredible aroma and flavours of the ripe fruit. They were thin-skinned and juicy, and when we bit into them, the sweet pulp and juice would run down our faces. We kids would get into trouble by starting tomato fights for fun. It astounds me to see tomatoes today that have no odour and skin so thick we have to use a knife to cut it.

Harvesting potatoes was back-breaking work. We stood on the runners of a potato digger, which had a big blade that dug up the plants and dropped them onto a metal belt that moved them upward. We would stand along the sides of the belt finding and throwing out clods and plant tops as the potatoes moved up the belt and dropped onto another belt, which pushed them into sacks at the back. After each long row, we would exchange positions so that no one got stuck on the hardest part of the digger, down by the blade, where we had to bend the farthest.

Our days would begin at 7:00 a.m. and end at 5:30 or 6:00, with a half-hour for lunch. We were paid 35 cents an hour for ten or more hours' work a day, often under a blazing sun, and yet I remember those days fondly because we were always making up little tricks to play on each other.

Celery was one of the toughest vegetables for me. We would bend over and pull up the plant, then trim off the roots with a curved blade. That was okay, but there was something in the leaves that would rub onto our bare arms, and I would develop what we called celery rash, large purple blisters that would take months to heal.

One year we lived on a peach farm, and I loved that. I was only eleven, but I got to drive a tractor pulling a flatbed onto which the pickers would load their baskets. The tractor was not speedy, and we didn't have to back up or shift gears, so even a kid could drive it. I would eat the luscious fruit all day until I got "fuzzitis," our name for a rash around the mouth from the tiny hairs on the peach skin. I often had to run behind the trees because I'd get the runs from eating so many peaches.

In 1947 we moved from the farm to Leamington, a town of about ten thousand people. Dad got a job in a dry cleaner's, because that's what he had done before the war. The owner of the dry cleaner's put us up in a house on an acre lot he owned. He suggested we go into partnership and grow onions on the lot. The owner would provide the land and everything we needed to grow the vegetables, and we would provide the muscle power. The profits would be split equally. Since Dad was working at the dry cleaner's full-time, it fell to my sisters and me to do the bulk of the work on the lot once the onions were in the ground. We had to weed and hoe and spread fertilizer, but it was always just play. Dad had dreams of making a killing and promised I would get enough money to buy a bike. That was incentive enough for me, and I spent the summer working my guts out on that one acre.

Finally the onions grew nice and plump, and we had to pull them up and lay them beside the rows so that the tops could dry out. One day while they were still drying, it poured rain. But eventually the rain stopped, and a few days later, we cut the tops off, graded the onions by size, bagged them, and sent them off to market. You can imagine my excitement as I anticipated my new bicycle.

A few days later, Dad came home looking sad. The rain had worked its way down the drying stalks and the onions had rotted in the centre. Most of them were worthless. The good ones had been separated out and sold, but the salvaged remnants didn't pay enough to cover costs. The owner lost money and we got nothing. Dad came to comfort me that night and slipped me a ten-dollar bill for that summer of effort. I cried bitterly that night because I had worked so hard but had "counted my chickens before they had hatched," and that was another life lesson.

A constant injunction from my mother was "Share, don't be greedy"—one more lesson from the Depression. All during my early childhood, before and after the war, weekends were spent with relatives as uncles, aunts, and cousins gathered at my grandparents' farm. Those gatherings were affirmation of the importance of family, but I realize in hindsight that a lot of the food grown on the farm was being shared out within the family.

But the notion that sharing was important extended beyond family. It was what we did. Whether it was with food or muscle power or talent, we never squawked when asked to help out. Sometimes during those years after the war when we were so poor, I would watch with puzzlement as my parents gave neighbours or visitors food we'd grown or fish we'd caught or treats Mom had baked. When they'd left, before I could ask why, Mom would say, "Don't begrudge your neighbours and friends, because you never know when you might need their help," a self-interested point of view but one that makes a lot of sense.

40 The Depression had given my parents a deep sense that we have to "live within our means," that we should always "save some for tomorrow." That seems so quaint and irrelevant today, when using credit cards and buying things on time (with a mortgage or loan) are so widespread. A friend told me a few years ago that it's better to go into debt because over time, inflation means that the payments get relatively cheaper and cheaper. That notion of deliberately going into debt makes me cringe the way I do when someone scrapes a fingernail across a blackboard.

When I was a boy, Mom and Dad would constantly tell us we were working hard because we needed the money to "buy the necessities." I don't know what your generation would consider a necessity, but for us it was food and clothes, then a stove, an icebox or a refrigerator, a bed and bedding, a radio, and cooking utensils like pots and pans. People were just beginning to think that telephones and cars were necessities too. So we were on the cusp of huge changes. In a society in which consumption is a sport, entertainment, or even our civic responsibility, it seems we work hard to fulfill our *wants,* not our *needs.* And there's no end to what we want.

When I was a kid, a car was a necessity to get from point A to point B quickly, not a statement of wealth or importance, and clothing was material to cover the naughty bits and to keep us warm in winter, dry in the rain, and cool in the summer sun—not a fashion statement. There were people who loved to flounce about in fancy new clothes and some who loudly showed off a new car, but we were taught to feel sorry for them because they seemed to feel these things made them better or more important than we were. "They've got onto the wrong road," my dad would say.

Perhaps it was just a way of justifying our poverty, but to this day, I try to teach you what my parents taught me. When the great economic collapse comes—and it will come during your lifetimes—you'll be better prepared for it by incorporating those values that the Great Depression taught my parents.

four

WHY DO SPORTS MATTER?

MY DARLING GRANDCHILDREN,

As you know, I take great joy in cheering for you when you participate in sports, whether it is soccer, hockey, or snowboarding. I spent many, many early-morning hours at the ice rink while Uncle Troy played hockey, and Ganhi, Tiis, and Ryo, I embarrassed your moms with my rabid cheering when they played basketball. I loved watching you play hockey, Midori and Tamo, but Tamo, your snowboarding stunts always terrified me.

I am a big spectating fan of certain sports, especially football and basketball. But I wasn't raised playing sports. When we were moved to the camps at Slocan shortly after the war began, there was no school for over a year because there was a shortage of trained teachers among the Japanese Canadian population. So I spent all my time roaming the lakeshore and the mountains around the camps. It was very remote country, and for a kid without any school, you can imagine what a magical playground it was. In the 1970s and early '80s, the area became a battleground over logging. The battles ended in 1983, when the mountains on the west side of Slocan Lake were declared to be Valhalla Provincial Park.

Once school started at the camp, I don't remember any organized sports or even formal phys-ed classes. During those years, few resources were available in such a remote place. When we moved to London, Ontario, in 1949, I was thirteen and Dad's emphasis was on school. He believed and taught us that the way out of our poverty was hard work and education. When he was mad at me, his worst threat was to pull me out of school.

My cousins Art and Dan were my age and had lived in London during the war, so they were completely integrated into the community. They also played football and basketball and were excellent athletes. I knew nothing about those sports. One time, my cousins needed another player for their touch football game and recruited me to play. I stood on the line without any idea what to do, so everyone ignored me. Consequently, no one bothered to cover me, and suddenly there I was, wide open. The quarterback threw the ball at me, and it bounced off my chest because I didn't even know how to catch the torpedo-shaped ball. My cousins never asked me to play again.

Life for me was going to school and coming straight home after classes to do homework or chores around the house. On weekends and during summer holidays, I worked for Suzuki Brothers Construction, a company my uncles had established to build houses. (I was amazed to learn in my civics class that most of the kids didn't work over the summer; they had holidays.) From shovelling gravel into cement mixers to hammering sheeting onto rafters to finish roofs, I loved working in construction. As always, every paycheck went straight to Mom.

Dad regarded playing sports as a frivolous activity because it meant time spent away from chores or work. He thought my cousins were wasting their time by playing sports and saw no irony in the fact that we spent a lot of time camping and fishing. So it never occurred to me to try out for any team. But at school, I would eat my lunch in the gym and watch kids play pickup basketball, which looked like a lot of fun. Eventually, I was tempted onto the court to shoot baskets and finally to play with a group of other nerds like me. Because I worked in construction, I was in great physical shape, and I found that I was coordinated too. Soon I started to play every noon hour after bolting down my lunch. Then I discovered volleyball and, finally, touch football. Now, as an old man looking back, I wish I had tried out for teams in high school, because I think I could have made them—but I didn't have a clue how to play the games properly or what the rules were.

Activities like tennis, swimming, and walking are great and can be continued into old age. But I also think team sports teach vital lessons about getting along with others, cooperating, and working together toward a goal. And there's something very primal and tribal about identifying with a team—we get so bound up in its fate that we can be at the height of elation or in the depths of despair for days, even weeks, after the victory or the defeat of our team.

Identifying with a team can also be a unifying factor, as we saw in the magnificent film *Invictus,* about Nelson Mandela and the South African rugby team. And as they say, "We can't have a healthy mind without a healthy body."

I see now that Dad was dead wrong: playing sports is a vital part of both growing up and adulthood. The most important aspect of playing sports of any kind is that it is fun, but it also keeps us active and makes us move our bodies. After all, that's what a body evolved for. Our evolutionary roots go back to the plains of Africa, where we often had to respond to threats or opportunities by hitting, grabbing, running, or climbing. We had to be in condition to survive. And when you think about it, exercising the body is how its parts stay strong. I mean, that's what lifting weights is about, isn't it?

We need to be active, so if there are sports that we enjoy doing, what better way to stay in shape? When you look at the profile of diseases of aging like diabetes, cancer, stroke, and Alzheimer's, the one common factor that reduces the risk for each of them is exercise. I tell the proprietor of the gym I go to that I don't go to bulk up and look good; rather, at my age, exercising is the best preventive medicine there is.

We don't think about that reality when we build the world around us. It's as if we want to eliminate every reminder of our biological needs. A car, for example, is a wonderful technology that enabled us to travel farther than we could by walking or even riding a horse. But we began to design our cities not to do what was best for us but to serve the automobile. Cars pushed bikes and public transit to the periphery so that our transportation system was primarily focused on serving private automobiles. In a time of cheap oil, we could use a car to take a quick trip to the grocer's or to visit a friend rather than walking or taking public transit. Not only have cars created pollution, they have made us less healthy. It may be convenient to drive a few blocks, but walking is a lot better for us—and besides, why are we always in a hurry?

{five}

MOTIVATION AND VALUES

MY DEAREST ONES,

I hope I don't get too preachy here when I talk to you about what drives us to do what we do and what values should motivate us. Well, I guess it's inevitable that I will sound kind of preachy, but you can ignore most of it or pick and choose what you think is useful in your lives. What sets people on their life course? It's a question I've often asked myself as I watch you grow older. Tamo, as the eldest of my grandchildren, your incredible athleticism in hockey, football, and snowboarding seemed to be leading you to some kind of career in sports. I was so surprised and so proud when you morphed into a snowboard activist trying to entice young boarders to notice the world around them and how they were affected by it and how they could make it better. Because of your Chilean roots, you could snowboard in

47

48

Canada during the winter and then continue snowboarding in Chile during our summer. As a result, you were exposed to issues of poverty in South America and to environmental concerns like the plight of sea turtles, and you have since gone on to become an environmental activist. I wonder where that will lead you in the coming years, but go for it!

We know about child prodigies who are found to have incredible talents at hockey or chess or piano. But how do they discover that talent? What encourages them to go on? The story of how Canadian hockey star Wayne Gretzky's father, Walter, would make a rink every winter so Wayne could play hockey is legendary, but what drove Wayne as a young boy to commit so much to the sport? It had to be fun, of course, but come on—for hours and hours?

Journalists often ask what led me to become an environmentalist. I never thought of environmentalism as a career, and when young people ask me how they can "save the world," I tell them not to worry about the world. The planet will do what it does with or without us. I tell them, "Follow your heart. Do what you love, whether it's art, music, writing, fixing cars, or carpentry." Environmentalism is not a specialty or a discipline like medicine or teaching or law. It's a way of seeing the world and recognizing that we are a part of the biosphere, dependent on nature—air, water, soil, photosynthesis, biodiversity—for our health and well-being, and we need everyone to see the world through that lens.

Our parents and the way they raise us tilt us toward what they are interested in and believe is important. When you look at religious affiliation or voting behaviour, for example, they follow family lines as if they're hereditary. If your parents are Catholic, Muslim, or Jewish, chances are you will adopt the same religion. It's the same with voting; despite a rebellious phase against parental values, chances are that as people grow older, they will probably vote for the same party as their parents. There are no genes for religious affiliation or political party, of course. But religion and socioeconomic group affect the way we see the world as much as gender and ethnicity influence the course we follow into life.

The overwhelming influence on my life was living in the camp during World War II. Because Mom had a job while Dad was away in a road camp, I ended up in the surrounding forests. And they were a magical place that had a profound effect on me. The river, lake, and forest were my escape, a refuge from the other kids, an enchanted place. Even today, when I enter a forest I am overcome by the emotions I felt as a child.

After Dad joined us in Slocan, he and I were soon hiking those mountains in search of lakes and creeks where we could fish. Decades later, Dad, Nana, your parents, and I retraced those hikes, and the fish are still there! The big difference is, as my father remarked, the trees are so much bigger. During the war, we depended on the fish we caught for food. We hiked up mountains overnight, and once made a lean-to that kept out the snow but reflected the heat from the fire onto us. Dad kept the fire going all night, and we were very comfortable in our sleeping bags. We didn't have tents, so we often slept in old log cabins built by miners or trappers. We clambered over immense treefalls and had to watch out for the spikes of devil's club.

Porcupines would come into the cabins and gnaw on paddles or anything that might have salt from sweat on it. Once when we got to a cabin and found a porcupine inside, Dad grabbed a sweater and began to hit the animal with it. It jumped around trying to escape as I begged Dad to stop. I thought he was hurting the porcupine, but he just wanted the quills to use as floats on our lines. In the fall, we would roam far and wide searching for the prized pine mushrooms (*matsutake*) that Japanese people adore for their aromatic smell and almost meatlike texture.

These experiences shaped me. Wilderness was a necessary part of my life, and I took all of my children out into the woods to camp and hike and fish from when they were infants. It has been a joy to me to see your parents take all of you out into the wilderness since you were babies. Jonathan, your physical handicaps have severely restricted your access to wilderness areas, but I know your parents have made a point of getting you out into canoes and to summer camps. One of my favourite pictures is of you in a canoe just laughing with pure joy. Remember when you came out to our cabin on Quadra Island and you caught a fish?

My parents didn't take me out into the bush so that I would become a forester, fisheries officer, or biologist. It was just a part of our lives that made us happy. But I don't think it is a surprise that I ended up studying biology.

My parents had lost everything during the war, and when we moved to Ontario, we started life from scratch—we had no savings, no household goods for the kitchen, living room, or bedrooms. But as I have said, I didn't think we were poor. I was surrounded by family; we always had love, basic clothing, housing, and food; and being a child, I never worried about how my parents were providing it all. It was taken for granted that we all had to work to earn money, whether it was working on a farm during the summer, babysitting, or working in construction after we moved to London, in 1949.

Thinking back, I realize Dad was wondering all that time what I might do when I was a man. When I was in my early teens and he emphasized how important it was to be able to speak extemporaneously, he suggested I think about becoming a minister in a church because I had a good, loud voice. Since I was an atheist, I never took him seriously. When he met a man in Leamington who was in the jewellery business, he got interested in how gems like diamonds were cut and urged me to go with him to watch so that I might consider becoming a diamond cutter. I had no interest at all, but now I realize it wasn't so much what I might do that concerned him but that I find a job that would be secure for life.

Dad constantly told me that I should always work hard at whatever I was doing. He hated a lackadaisical attitude toward work. "You only get out of it what you're willing to put into it," he admonished. I knew that since he was Japanese, he had to work harder than white people just to get the same pay. But he also wanted, by working hard, to prove that

Canada had made a mistake in treating us so badly during the war. My parents were always concerned about security—security from debt, security in health, security in work. The very idea of ever going on welfare was totally repugnant to my parents, a sign of some character flaw, a lack of pride, or laziness. I find it astonishing and unacceptable to try to make a lot of money through some kind of clever scheme or by seeking a job just because it pays well. Sure, it's great if a job pays well, but if you're going to spend more than half your waking hours doing it, it should provide something more than just money—either enjoyment or contribution to society. I am so glad your parents have the same sense and that none of you is obsessed with running after money.

It may sound weird, but I enjoyed whatever I worked at, and believe me, some of it was pretty difficult—try tarring a concrete foundation in a narrow trench when the temperature is 35°C, navigating along floor joists covered in ice at subzero temperatures, or shovelling eleven or twelve truck-loads of gravel into a concrete mixer for a foundation. Or for that matter, as I did after I became a scientist, looking at thousands of fruit flies through a microscope for hours on end, day and night, day after day.

You may know that ever since I married Nana, I have been the dishwasher in the family. I made a promise to her, and that's my job. And I enjoy it. I enjoy taking a huge pile of dirty dishes and pots, scrubbing my way through them, and leaving them clean and shiny. I guess it's just about a person's attitude toward a task. At the cabin on Quadra, our septic system has backed up a couple of times, and I've loved watching the plumber suit up in a rubber outfit and enter the tank to fix it. It's a very smelly job but one that we are so grateful is being done, and I know that if I had the skill, I would gain a lot of satisfaction doing it too.

When Severn and Sarika were still girls (I think about eleven and eight years old, respectively), we went on a rafting trip down the Babine River. It was to be a no-impact camping trip, meaning that during the ten-day trip, we would leave nothing behind—no garbage, no ashes from fires, no toilet paper, no feces. We had a portable potty and pooped into a plastic bag. Each day, the poop had to be squeezed to the bottom of the bag, which would then be knotted up and put into a barrel with a tight lid. Someone had to do it, usually one of the river guides, but I volunteered for the job because I wanted the girls to see that no one should think they are too good to do the most menial task. And it wasn't a horrible experience.

In the 1950s, when I went to high school, perhaps 10 percent of kids went from high school to university, and kids who liked science or were good at it often aimed to go into medicine. I got good grades because my parents constantly emphasized that the way for us to "get ahead" (whatever that meant) was through hard work and education. So I expected to go into medicine, not because I loved medicine or wanted to serve humanity, but because that's what top students did, especially if they were good in science. I didn't even think much about what it would mean to be a doctor.

Back in those days, in Ontario, we went through grade 13 before going to university. If you had good marks, you could be accepted into medical school at the end of the second year of university. I went to school in the United States, but since we lived in London, which was home to the University of Western Ontario (now called Western University), I dropped into Western at the end of my second year to visit the dean of Medicine. He assured me that with my grades and academic record, I would have no trouble getting into medicine there. But in my third year of honours Biology, I had to take a course in genetics. I was hooked. For the first time in my life, I couldn't wait to get to the next class. I found the mathematical elegance and precision of genetics fascinating, and Bill Hexter, the professor, was a masterful teacher who unfolded the solving of mysteries of heredity like a detective story. There was no turning back. I wanted to become a geneticist and wrote the dean at Western that I had decided not to pursue medicine. My mother was especially disappointed that I turned down a chance to be a medical doctor in order to study fruit flies, but I never regretted it.

FROM MY POSITION now as an elder and your grandpa, I can say that I have learned a lot from my mistakes, failures, and successes. The most important piece of advice I can offer is please do not shape your life around making money, acquiring power, or becoming famous. These ends may be the consequence of working toward something that is important to you, but they should not be your goal. What do you believe in? What do you enjoy? That should guide you in life. If by chance you do achieve money, power, or fame, 55 they will not bring real joy, pride, or satisfaction. And too often people who aspire to those goals will sacrifice friends, even family, trying to achieve them. But when they become rich, famous, and powerful, what do they stand for? What are their values? These are the important questions.

AFTER I MADE the decision to become a geneticist and then completed my PhD in genetics, I received a number of offers from American universities. They were tempting, but I decided I did not want to live permanently in the United States, not because Canada was superior, but because it was different, and the difference mattered to me. To me, Canada meant Tommy Douglas, the socialist CCF party that later became the NDP, medicare, Quebec, a balance of payments system whereby the well-off provinces shared some of their good fortune with have-not provinces, the National Film Board, and the Canadian Broadcasting Corporation. Those were some of the fundamental differences that I treasured and that allowed me to make a commitment to this nation.

But I was a trained geneticist and anxious to make my name in the field when I obtained a university position back in Canada. So how did the environment come to dominate my life?

That reality happened when I became interested in television journalism. And I was first attracted to television because I felt it was important to inform and educate people about the repercussions of powerful new ideas and applications from science and technology. I was extremely fortunate to land in the orbit of Jim Murray, the executive producer of *The Nature of Things*. He was strongly influenced by John Livingston, a former executive producer of the show and professor of environmental studies at York University. Livingston had an uncompromising biocentric view; he saw humans as one species among many on Earth—not as the centre of everything and the most important species, but as a part of and dependent on the rest of nature. Most people see humans as the centre of the universe. This is known as the anthropocentric view, and a long time ago I used to see us that way too.

I remember arguing with Jim, who said every species had just as much of a right to live as we did and so we fight to keep them from going extinct for *their* sake. I responded that a right is a human-created concept that doesn't exist in nature. Because we consider other life-forms important to us, each extinction diminishes *us*. I'm embarrassed by that argument now, although I do say we must preserve ecosystems and protect all species because it's in our self-interest—not just for aesthetic or philosophical reasons, as real and important as those are, but because life is the fount of our lives; our survival and well-being depend on *nature's* survival and well-being.

Jim would also be distressed if after we did a story I became passionate about it and couldn't just move on.

When we reported on the Amazon, I met the remarkable Kaiapo leader Paulinho Paiakan, who galvanized me with his struggle to protect his territory. Nana and I ended up raising money for him and visiting him in his village. We also brought him and his family to stay with us when his enemies threatened to kill him. When we did a story on the Cree of Quebec and their fight against the huge dams that were flooding their territory, I ended up narrating a film for them, speaking out on their behalf at rallies, and visiting their communities. Over and over, I championed causes that were brought to my attention by our programs. My work on these issues took up time and detracted from my own work, but it gave me a sense that I was working for ecological or social issues that mattered to me. So in the end, it was selfish of me because I gained satisfaction from doing something I felt was important, and I was fortunate to have both a platform to spread ideas and a boss whose worldview was closely aligned with mine.

Whatever you do, do it to the best of your ability and make sure it aligns with your deepest values. I meet people who apologize because they work for salmon farms, on the Alberta tar sands, or for a pharmaceutical corporation or logging company. They say they don't agree with their employers but they have to make a living. I hope none of you finds yourself in a situation where your job clashes with your beliefs.

I owe a lot to my father for bringing me up with a strong sense that I must speak out and act on my beliefs. He warned me that if I wanted everyone to like me, I wouldn't stand for anything because there would always be people who disagreed with me. He had contempt for people who wouldn't speak up because they were afraid of the repercussions.

Dad was a most unusual man. I loved to listen to him tell stories of his childhood. He was the oldest child in a family of seven children and thus was expected to be the role model for his younger siblings. As with most immigrants, making money and having financial security were his parents' driving principles. But Dad was a dreamer. He told me that when he was a boy, he found he could catch sticklebacks in a small net. I guess it was fun, so he kept catching more and more and stuffing them into a bottle. To his surprise, they all died. That was the first time he realized that fish needed enough water to live.

He also told me how he would watch wasps collecting balls of mud to make their nests. "You know, David," he said, "I saw there was some kind of parasite on them that looked like a tiny lobster." At the time, I was a professor at the University of British Columbia (UBC), so I nodded politely and patronizingly. Later I discovered that indeed there are parasites of insects that do look like little crustaceans.

When Dad was five, his mother took him to Japan, intending to leave him there to be educated as a Japanese. He didn't want to stay there, so he wouldn't let her out of his sight. When she disappeared, he would start howling. His grandparents didn't want this crybaby and made her take him back to Canada. But while he was in Japan, he watched how people processed nori (seaweed) by chopping the seaweed into small pieces, making those pieces into a slurry, and then passing a screen through the slurry so that the seaweed could be picked up in a thin sheet. He had amazing powers of observation and memory. He would also lie on the ground and actually watch bamboo shoots grow. 59

His father was a boatbuilder, and one time he took Dad on a boat to Gambier Island, in Howe Sound, not far from Vancouver. While my grandfather was doing business, Dad could play. Even though he was a boy, Dad was fascinated by the miniature arbutus trees with smooth red bark growing on rock like bonsai. So he carefully dug them out and filled a bucket with them to take home and plant. When his dad came down to the boat, he threw away the bucket full of plants without even asking what they were for. When Dad told me this, I could see it still hurt him that his father thought what he did was a waste of time.

On weekends, when we would go to my grandparents' place, I often heard my grandfather chastising my father for "wasting time" by going camping or fishing instead of working and making money. I appreciated that Dad had not lived up to his father's wish that he be a role model for his younger siblings. I would tease Dad by calling him a "mutant," since he was so different from the obedient child he was supposed to be. I was glad he was a mutant.

He was naturally curious and would always get people to talk about themselves. Since we all love to talk about ourselves, they would think he was a terrific guy. And he was. But Dad had his shortcomings. He was very generous and would give anything if a person was interested—fishing gear, fish, vegetables, whatever—even though we were never wealthy, and I often felt he did it for show.

60

In hindsight, I realize his generosity established a network of people who were often just as generous in return. This is what makes the potlatch such a powerful cohesive force among west coast First Nations. But when Dad gave a person something but was not thanked or acknowledged fully, Dad never forgot and always held it against that person—a bad trait that I inherited. Still, I admire Dad's generosity and try to emulate it in sharing my good fortune. It's why Nana and I have tried to involve you all in gathering food for Christmas hampers that we deliver to the Salvation Army. We feel it's important for you to know how fortunate you are and that the joy of Christmas is as much in sharing as it is in receiving.

AFTER RENÉ LÉVESQUE was elected the first separatist premier of Quebec, I worried about the real possibility that Canada might be broken up. Quebec is a huge part of what I love about Canada, and I did not want to see it become a separate nation. But what could we do way out in British Columbia? Nana and I decided that at least we could learn French so that in any interactions with a Québécois person, we could speak in their language. So I took Tamiko, Troy, and my young bride, your nana, to Chicoutimi, in Quebec, for six weeks of total immersion.

Chicoutimi is the heart of separatist country, so everyone there was going to speak to us in French. Nana and I were the only adults in our class. The rest were teenagers who were on school programs to learn French. We were billeted with three families—two different ones for Tamiko and Troy, while Nana and I were together with one family, thank goodness. We spent the days with teachers and on trips. It was a great experience.

At the end of our stay, we had an evening of celebration with our hosts and teachers. Nana and I wrote a play (in French, of course) based on the Frankenstein story. In our play, two people, one French and the other English, are sewn together by Dr. Frankenstein in an experiment. When the two wake up and discover they are physically linked, they begin to fight (in English and French) and finally demand to be cut apart. All the French–English problems of Canada are articulated by the two characters, who, in exasperation, want to be separated. We ended the play with the doctor explaining that together they combine the power of two and will be much stronger than either alone. There was nothing subtle about the play, and deep in the heart of separatist Quebec, I thought it was pretty nervy. We got a standing ovation from the Québécois audience.

While we were preparing for the evening, Tara (your Nana) and I were running around making sure folks knew their lines, checking the costumes and the operating-room scenery, and memorizing our own lines. One of the kids from the class was surprised that we were taking it all so seriously. "Why?" I asked. To which he replied, "It's just a nothing concert. Like, who cares?" I was stunned because the fun was in all the running around and doing the best we could.

I am so pleased that each of you is learning from your parents, who always throw themselves into whatever they do. Tamo and Midori, both your parents enthusiastically supported your sports abilities and loved taking you winter camping. Ganhi and Tiis, your parents always go all out, whether it's fishing or camping, preparing a feast, or working to preserve the Haida language. Jonathan, your parents worked tirelessly to maximize your physical and mental abilities and for you to become an expert at using computers. And Ryo, look at your parents, both raising you and working to get their PhDs at the same time! I am so proud of them but also so pleased that they are such great role models for you to follow.

{*six*}

MY LIFE IN MEDIA

MY ANGELS,

Pardon me for continually talking about the past, but that's what most of these letters are about, and in this time of enormous and rapid change, I believe that elders have a special role in reminding people of what once was. The rate and scale of change today are staggering. Take mobile phones, for example. New models are coming out all the time, with more bells and whistles that stimulate a rush to get the latest offering. I'm always astounded to see the long lineups for the latest models of iPhones, as well as laptops and computer games.

Because I am a teacher and scientist, communication has been a major activity in my life. As I've said, Dad always felt that to do well in Canadian society, one had to be able to speak in public, so he trained me as an orator. When I taught in university, I mimicked the way I had prepared for oratorical contests when I was young, writing out my lectures longhand, then practising out loud, often in the shower, and driving my family mad.

I took pride in teaching, especially in the early years, when my classes were small and I could see when students were confused or when they suddenly "got it." I never used slides or audiovisual aids; I used the blackboard, because as I wrote, I gave students time for an idea to sink in. I've often listened to lecturers who use PowerPoint to show slides, then proceed to read what's on the slides! Why give a talk about something that can be handed out on a sheet? I find that drawing a graph or picture or writing words provides time for students to think about the ideas or processes being presented, so long as they aren't madly trying to copy what I'm writing or drawing—that's what I hand out to them.

Today when I visit classes, I am astounded by the technology, which, I have to admit, can be a superb aid to teaching. I think that, in my area, seeing chromosomes line up and split during cell division or graphic animation of DNA replicating or being read is better than words or crude drawings. I cannot imagine teaching today, but still, I do wonder how engaged a student can be when a class becomes like watching a TV show. A lecture is powerful when the presenter loves the subject and conveys excitement, joy, and especially passion. I always took pride in my lectures because I love genetics so much. In fact, I was kind of arrogant about being a good speaker until I heard Harvard's Nobel Prize winner George Wald give a lecture to undergrads.

I had heard that he was considered one of the greatest lecturers in the school's history, and when I heard him, I could see why. He was passionate, insightful, and humorous, and he completely captivated me and set a standard I always tried afterward to emulate.

In a lecture, I am engaged in presenting ideas, and even when there is a large audience, I want people to focus on me to make it seem that I am talking to each of them personally. I believe that what one gets out of communication is directly proportional to the amount of effort expended. So print—books, articles, columns—is by far the most effective medium for transferring an idea. For one thing, when you are reading, you can control the speed with which you acquire information simply by slowing down or speeding up. You can also go over a section again and again. But you have to work to get the meaning.

After print, radio is next most effective because, again, listeners have to exert effort and create the images to go with the words in their minds. Radio is the medium I do best at and enjoy the most. Radio interviews are intimate conversations that can be rich in humour, self-deprecation, and emotion. I love the cut and thrust of a real exchange. Television is overpowering because we are such visual creatures, but it is much more contrived than radio. Usually a single camera is used on a shoot, so what is presented as a dialogue is actually a film of the response of an interviewee, and then the camera is repositioned to film the interviewer, with "re-asks" (where the questions posed in the interview are asked again) and "reaction shots" (often called "noddies," because the interviewer is filmed nodding and reacting to the interviewee, who is usually gone). The two sets of films are then edited so that to the viewer of the show, it seems there were cameras recording both at once.

66

I had always thought that on programs like *The Nature of Things,* we were offering a picture of nature that would seduce people into loving the real world we share with other species. But on reflection, I realized we were also creating images of nature that were *better* than the real world. We send wildlife filmmakers to remote places like the Arctic or the Amazon, where they spend weeks and months trying to get the best shots—polar bears emerging from a den, capturing seals, or swimming from ice floes in the Arctic, or flocks of parrots, capybaras, snakes, and jaguars in the Amazon. Then one breathtaking shot after another is edited together so that months of effort are boiled down to a few minutes of action. Technology provides images of nature not possible to see in real time with the naked eye. Microscopy, time lapse, high-definition, drones, submarines, endoscopes—the list of technological innovations for filming is remarkable.

But anyone expecting to visit the Arctic or the Amazon to witness the hyperactivity seen on *The Nature of Things* will be disappointed. In the Amazon rainforest, much of the activity takes place at night or in the canopy high above the forest floor. Nature needs time to reveal her secrets, but we are an impatient animal. In a world where satellite dishes and cable deliver dozens of channels from which to choose, my shows have to compete for the attention of remote-control-clutching viewers who have the attention span of a hummingbird. We don't have the luxury of time to relish the gradual revelations in nature, and the impression we get from films and TV is of nature hopped up on steroids.

Still, as long as we realize that the vital ingredient of time is left out, I believe that natural-history films convey a sense of wonder, amazement, and love that we desperately need if we are to appreciate the role nature plays in our lives.

The bread and butter of *The Nature of Things,* the thing the series cut its teeth on and is beloved for, is natural history. I've always maintained that people have an innate love of nature, that we could get an audience for a show on the sex life of an oyster if it was shot and edited well. Our problem today is choice. There is simply too much of it. I have only been in a Walmart store once, when I was in Prince George, British Columbia, and needed a specific item for a camping trip. I was overwhelmed by the aisles of things I didn't know even existed, let alone were needed. I left without finding what I wanted because there was simply too much to wade through.

And that's how I feel about TV programs today. Not only can we choose from hundreds of channels on satellite, we can also roam across the Internet and find endless fascinating material. The first time I decided to look at YouTube, I wanted to see if there was film about a remarkable phenomenon I had heard of in hagfish: when they are agitated, they secrete a material that puffs up like jelly, clearly a protective mechanism against predation. I was astonished to find many videos to select from. After looking at a couple, I was presented with more videos on related topics that looked interesting, so I opened a couple of them. I was still watching videos with fascination when I realized that hours had passed! Yes, that world is endlessly fascinating, but it's pure entertainment. It reminds me of an old science show called *What Will They Think of Next?* that portrayed science almost as a magic show with scientists as the magicians. This is not my notion of how to demystify science or to make it more accessible to the general public. The Internet gives me the impression that I can be constantly surprised and amazed at peoples' stupidity, bravery, ability—you name it, you google it, and you'll find something.

But when will we find time for each other, or time to go outside and simply be, or just to think or be happy? It is so sad to see groups of people in which many are looking at or watching their cellphone. Even couples who I assume are on a date are often each on their phones.

Today, radical innovation and multiple changes can spread through society in months. But often unintended consequences result because not enough consideration has been given to the potential impact of new ideas.

Over my lifetime, so much has changed in the area of communication. My father told me that when he was a boy, he would make "crystal sets" that he could listen to as a radio. Electricity was not required, because the energy of a radio signal was propagated through a long wire antenna that carried the signal to a crystalline material that, I suppose, vibrated and could be heard.

If we consider Dad's lifetime as an extension of my experience, it encompasses electronic communication from early radio days. When I was a boy, radios had a series of vacuum tubes that burned out and had to be periodically replaced. When I was about ten years old, I contracted measles and had to stay home in isolation. The curtains in my room were all drawn, apparently to protect my light-sensitive eyes. I only remember long hours lying in the dark room listening to the radio. I got caught up in long-running radio series—*Our Gal Sunday, Inner Sanctum, The Lone Ranger,* and many others. There were movies back then as well, and teenagers filled the seats at Saturday matinees to watch regular features like *Movietone News,* cartoons, and series like the Hopalong Cassidy pictures, which ran every weekend.

We moved to Leamington, Ontario, in 1946. Our next-door neighbours were living in the foundation of an unbuilt house, a basement that was covered by floor joists and sub-floor and coated with tar paper. The rest of the house was built over years—as they acquired the money, I assume. One day I was playing with the boy next door, and he told me he couldn't spend money on candy or soda pop because his family was saving up to buy a television set. I laughed and laughed at him because that sounded like the stupidest thing I had ever heard. I thought his parents had tricked him into believing something that I thought would never actually happen. Stupid me.

We moved to London in 1949, when the population was about seventy thousand, a big city in those days. Television was coming, and a few people owned sets. You could tell which house had TV because it would have a huge antenna on the roof to intercept signals from across the border in Detroit or Cleveland, since there was no station in London. It was a big deal to watch a television program, and I remember sitting with a large group in front of a TV set in someone's living room. But the images were like shadows, with lots of what was called "snow"—electronic blotches that further obscured the already faint pictures. The sound was all right, but I just couldn't see what the fuss was about.

When I left for college in the fall of 1954, none of the Suzuki family owned a television set. Tuition and room and board at Amherst College in Massachusetts were very high, and it was only because I received a scholarship that I could go. I bussed tables on the morning shift to earn extra money, and with studies and socializing on top of that, I had no time to watch television anyway. When I went off to graduate school in Chicago, I was married to your grandmother, Tamo, Midori, and Jonathan, and we had an unplanned baby (Tamiko). It was an intense time. I took care of the baby during the day while Joane worked, and then I went to the lab to work on my research through the night. It paid off when I finished my degree in less than three years. When we arrived at the Oak Ridge National Laboratory in Oak Ridge, Tennessee, for my postdoctoral year, in 1961, we stayed in a furnished rental house, and it had a television set! Joane may have watched television, but I was at the lab day and night, including weekends, and so just never got into watching it.

In 1962, I took a job at the University of Alberta, where I 71 worked the same kind of hours I had at Oak Ridge. The university produced a half-hour weekly TV program called *Your University Speaks,* in black and white. I don't even know what station it was broadcast on, but I suspect it was the CBC. It was shown on Sunday mornings, I think around 8:00. Anyway, somehow someone heard I gave good lectures, and so I was invited to present a lecture on aspects of genetics for the show. In the studio, there was just a big camera pointing at me and a screen with a rear projector to show slides. And that was it. I imagined that I was talking to my father, who was always interested in what I was doing but demanded that I explain things to him so that he could understand them. He had no patience for jargon or complex technical detail. "I'm not stupid, but explain it in English," he would chastise me if I got too technical and didn't get my point across.

As I pictured Dad on the other end of the camera, I found that the technology didn't intimidate me and the lecture came easily. To my surprise, Guy Vaughn, the producer, was delighted with my performance and invited me back the next week. I think I even got an honorarium of fifteen or twenty dollars for that show. I ended up doing eight shows, my very first television series.

After I had done three or four programs, I was walking to campus one day when someone accosted me and said, "I saw your show last week. I really liked it." I was flabbergasted to find that people actually watched television on a Sunday morning. I didn't, and never saw a single one of my own programs. I stuttered a thank-you, but my brain was in turmoil because I wanted to ask, "Why on earth are you watching television at that time of day?" In the ensuing weeks, a few students and even faculty members said they had caught one of my episodes, and I realized that although I didn't watch much television, a lot of people did. Even on a Sunday morning. After I moved to Vancouver, someone at CBC heard I had a bit of television experience, and so I was asked to come on different shows now and then to comment on a new discovery, technology, or book.

I had been shocked at how poorly scientists in Canada were funded compared with our American peers. My first grant was so small that I started thinking seriously about returning to the United States. Ironically, what enabled me to resist going back there was a large research grant I got from the U.S. Atomic Energy Commission, probably because I had spent a year at Oak Ridge. But I felt that if Canadians were going to support science adequately, they had to understand how science was relevant to their lives. So I suggested to Keith Christie, a CBC producer in Vancouver, that someone should do a science program for television. Although Toronto was the centre of the universe for English-language programming, the CBC did try to let the regions do some work. So Keith proposed a science show with me as the host. At that time Knowlton Nash was both an on-air news reader and head of programming, and he approved Keith's request. It would be a half-hour show on Sunday afternoon. Not as bad as early Sunday morning, perhaps, but it would be right up against Sunday football. Nevertheless, I was excited at the prospect of a national science show.

As the broadcast date approached, Knowlton called Keith to ask him how the show was going. "Which one?" Keith asked, and Knowlton replied, "You know, that one with Suzuki on science." And with that, Knowlton had named the show—*Suzuki on Science.*

The program debuted in 1970. The year before, I had gone to teach a course at the University of California at Berkeley. There was still tremendous campus foment over the Free Speech Movement and Vietnam, drugs, and flower power— a glorious time to be in the Bay area. I went to Berkeley as a straitlaced professor with short hair and horn-rimmed glasses and returned to Vancouver in granny glasses, long hair, and a headband, which became my trademark.

Suzuki on Science was what was called a "talking heads" program, with me interviewing scientists—essentially radio with pictures. (I find it interesting that many radio talk shows are now filming interviews and then broadcasting them on television.) I think I got paid fifty dollars a show. Money was never an issue for me; I wanted to get ideas out to the general public. We had a tiny budget, which we hoarded by doing most of the shows in the Vancouver studio. We saved the money for two big trips, one down the east coast and one down the west coast, where we could

interview scientists in top universities and research institutions. I don't know what the ratings were, but the series
developed a kind of cult following among young people who
identified with the "freak" who was the host (me). I know
some scientists who were outraged that a "hippie" like me
was posing as a scientist on the show.

I enjoyed doing the series and was delighted to get some
top scientists to share their work with the public. But there
was another long-running series—*The Nature of Things*—that
had a large and loyal audience, had a much bigger budget,
and was doing the kinds of visually spectacular programs
that were more appropriate for television than my talking
heads. After all, television's advantage over radio is pictures.
So after two seasons, I asked for more money to produce our
series or I was finished. The money never came, so I went
back to working full-time in the lab. I had no regrets and no
aspirations to do more shows for TV. I had tried and done my
thing on air, but research was still my great passion and my
lab was doing very exciting work, so I went back at science
wholeheartedly.

I had met Jim Murray and his partner, Nancy Archibald,
once in Toronto. Jim was executive producer and Nancy was
a producer of *The Nature of Things*, a series on nature, science,
and technology that had been started in 1960. I didn't realize
then how competitive Jim was, and only later learned that
he was checking me out as a competitor. I felt like a country bumpkin who knew nothing about serious television

programming and was just dabbling in it on a show with a tiny budget.

When Jim became executive producer of a prestigious series based on the bestselling book *The National Dream,* about the building of the transcontinental railway, with Pierre Berton, its author, as host, Nancy took over as executive producer of *The Nature of Things. The National Dream* was a ratings triumph, and after it was completed, Jim created a new science series called *Science Magazine,* which would present shorter reports, from two to five per show.

As different producers began to put together a variety of short stories for *Science Magazine,* Jim realized that a host was needed to make the transition from one item to another unrelated one. He ended up offering me the job, so in 1974 I took a leave from the University of British Columbia to go to Toronto to host my first big-budget national science program. I learned one of the most important lessons about public life when I took on that position. When *The National Dream* became a huge success, Jim could have gone on up the corporate ladder of CBC, but his love was science and natural history, and he chose to go back to it.

I still had a big lab when I was asked to host *Science Magazine,* but it was exciting to think of working with a top-notch executive producer on a series with a much bigger budget than we had when I had hosted *Suzuki on Science* a few years earlier. As we began to film different stories, I found the process of filming, then later, editing, tedious and boring. On one of the earliest shoots for *Science Magazine,* we went to New Orleans to film in a lab. I was seated on a stool as the camera assistant brought in the camera and tripod and set it up. The cameraman then set about making the lab "look like a lab," which always made me chuckle. Apparently an actual working lab that doesn't have test tubes bubbling with different-coloured liquids doesn't look like a real lab, at least for a television audience. As the lab was being rearranged, the soundman put a wire down my shirt and arranged the microphone, then asked me to say a few words so he could adjust the recording machine. A lighting man came in and began to set up lights that didn't show in the shot and then adjusted the filters and the focus of the light as the cameraman directed. Finally, when all seemed right, the cameraman came up and put a light meter beside my nose, took a reading, and went back to the camera and adjusted the focus. Then he came back and took another light reading and adjusted the focus. Nothing had changed. He did it a third time, then a fourth and fifth time! Finally I said, "For Christ's sake, shoot the damn thing!" Jim came over, grabbed my shoulder, dragged me into a side room, and shut the door. "Listen, Suzuki," he said. "Everyone in that room is busting their ass to make you look good. And that's not easy."

I slunk back into the room feeling very ashamed and never, ever got up on my high horse like that again. You see, he was absolutely right. When a program is broadcast, viewers don't say, "Wow, every shot was in focus" or "Wasn't the lighting great?" or "The sound was so crisp." They say, "Wasn't

Suzuki's show great?" I get all the credit for what is the work of literally dozens of people, from researchers, writers, and secretaries to editors, publicists, and a host of others work- ing to make programs and get them to air. I feel that way about everything I've done, from research in which students, postdocs, and colleagues all contribute to the work that comes out to books I've written and co-written and my work at the David Suzuki Foundation with its dozens of staff, hundreds of volunteers, and thousands of donors. I get an inordinate amount of credit for what is the result of the passion, commitment, and hard work of so many others. I feel an enormous responsibility to them, which is to do the very best I can in whatever I'm involved in and to be as credible and true to what I say as I can.

Science Magazine was scheduled to run for half a year in its inaugural season. It captured a younger audience and attracted 50 percent more viewers than *The Nature of Things*. The items were shorter and zippier, the kind young people prefer, so the series did very well. But CBC brass weren't committed to the idea of science programs, and before we had finished broadcasting all our shows, Knowlton Nash informed us it would be a one-season series. I was devastated.

At the end of the last show, I thanked the audience for joining us, then announced matter-of-factly that this was the last of the series and said goodbye. I assumed that was it, but apparently the CBC was deluged with phone calls and letters protesting the cancellation of the series, and within a few weeks, Knowlton told us it would carry on. So don't ever think letters and phone calls are a waste of time. They can work if there are enough of them.

78

The same people who produced *The Nature of Things* were also used for *Science Magazine.* After five successful seasons of *Science Magazine,* we agreed it would be great to combine *The Nature of Things* and *Science Magazine* into a single one-hour program, *The Nature of Things with David Suzuki.* Jim took over as executive producer of this new version of the series, and I felt honoured to be tied to a venerable series that had established such a high level of quality and a loyal following.

In the first year of *Science Magazine,* Diana Filer, a distinguished radio producer and executive, approached me with a proposal to host a brand-new one-hour science show for radio called *Quirks and Quarks.* I was intrigued and agreed to try.

For the first show, we attended the annual meeting of the American Association for the Advancement of Science (AAAS), a huge gathering of scientists that has the express purpose of communicating with media and the public. Hundreds of scientists, from Nobel laureates to hotshot young grad students, would give talks and speak to the press. Diana would line up people to meet with me, and I'd interview one scientist after another. It was an exhausting but great way to generate more than one show's worth of material—we could stockpile interviews and sprinkle them throughout the year. We did this every year, and these interviews continue to this day. The next year, we included interviews from the British Association for the Advancement of Science (BAAS), and that practice also continues today.

Jim was always protective of my time because he didn't want other things to distract me from his show. I knew he wasn't happy when I accepted projects outside of *The Nature of Things,* although he never protested. He happened to be in Vancouver when the first program of *Quirks and Quarks* was to be broadcast, so I invited him over to listen to it. I was excited about and proud of what we had done, and Jim was politely complimentary as the show proceeded. But about halfway through the program, I thought some of the voices, including mine, sounded a little higher than I remembered. Sure enough, something had gone wrong, and the tape was speeding up so that by the end, everyone sounded like the Chipmunks. I was horrified, but Jim was rolling on the floor laughing, and his mirth was not without a bit of satisfaction for my comeuppance.

In the four years I hosted *Quirks and Quarks,* we tried all kinds of things; after all, it was new territory. I went to New York City and spent a couple of days with Isaac Asimov, renowned as a science and science-fiction writer. He was a delightful man with an incredible drive to publish. I got him to talk about different science words or fields, and he would expound for three or four minutes on each. We included one Asimov item per show. Every week we featured a physicist, Jearl Walker, from Ohio; then Harlan Ellison, another famous science-fiction writer; and Terry Dickinson, who talked about astronomy. For a couple of years, we featured inventors with new devices. But again and again, our bread and butter was exciting stories at the cutting edge of different fields. Science is fascinating to the public so long as it is jargon free.

I was once taken in completely by an interview with a "scientist" who was in fact a CBC radio producer. Posing as a researcher, he described his project to catch a gigantic pre-historic shark he believed still existed by dragging a cow through the water as bait. He sucked me right in as I pursued his ideas, until finally, when I asked if he had had any success, he quipped, "Yes, I've caught the biggest fish of all—you. April Fool, Dr. Suzuki."

One of my most satisfying experiences was interviewing a British Nobel Prize–winning physiologist at the BAAS meeting. He did a fine job talking about his research but then veered into a discussion of his concerns about the degradation of the human gene pool. He had no idea I was a scientist, let alone a geneticist, and I let him go on. Finally, I suggested that Walter Bodmer, an eminent geneticist at Oxford, had shown that until racism was totally eliminated, comparisons between different racial groups to determine hereditary components of intelligence couldn't be made. I knew he would know who Bodmer was, and his pompous demeanour changed as he stood up to say he had a pressing engagement. I didn't let him go without first telling him that claims of a hereditary basis for racial differences in intelligence had wide-reaching social ramifications and that as a Nobel Prize winner whose words would have an enormous impact, he had a responsibility to know what he was talking about. He left very quickly.

I loved *Quirks and Quarks* because radio is so much more my medium than television. When I started with *Suzuki on Science,* we filmed in-studio with two-inch videotape. When we went on location, we shot on 16 mm film, which was expensive, and each roll allowed only ten minutes of time. So we had to get what we wanted as efficiently as possible, in contrast to radio, where I could chat away to warm up a guest and explore avenues that I hadn't expected if any opened up. We could be funny or quirky and tell jokes because audiotape is cheap and editing is easy. For me, radio is natural and comfortable.

I am so proud to have hosted *Quirks and Quarks* for four years and to have shown that there is a big audience for science programs, that a science show can be funny, exciting, and relevant, and that there is always new material. Early on, a person in communications at UBC warned me that I would have a hard time finding enough stories to fill an hour of programming every week, but the reality is that I could have done an hour a night if I'd had the budget and the staff, because there was no shortage of material. My preference, though, would be for stories involving some aspect of science to be a part of programming in news and current affairs, not hived off as a special-interest area. *Quirks and Quarks* very quickly established a solid audience and is now a venerable part of radio programming, just as *The Nature of Things* has been in television.

From 1975 to 1979, I hosted both *Science Magazine* on television and *Quirks and Quarks* on radio. While I preferred doing radio, it turned out that doing weekly shows demanded my constant involvement and took much more of my time than *Science Magazine* did. I was still teaching at UBC and had an active research group, and I knew when we decided to amalgamate *Science Magazine* and *The Nature of Things* that the hour-long program would be a bigger burden. The audience for *The Nature of Things* would be much larger, and I felt we could explore issues more deeply, so I reluctantly chose to leave *Quirks and Quarks*. But I remain delighted and proud that it is such a big part of CBC's radio offerings and has had very good hosts.

In my early years with *The Nature of Things*, our main competitors were the Canadian private network CTV and the American networks CBS, NBC, and ABC. I learned that ratings mattered even though CBC is a public broadcaster, but *The Nature of Things* had a good audience average—well over a million a night. Over the years, as cable and satellite dishes brought more choice to viewers and remote controls made them more skittish, our audiences began to fall. And in competing for viewers, we had to be louder, sexier, more sensational, and faster paced.

I always decried the short attention span we catered to on television. If nature needs time to reveal her secrets, I would say, why don't we give her some of that time on our programs, putting in "dead air" instead of trying to pack in more jolts per minute? Give the viewer an understanding of nature's pace.

I found out that my own notion of time had changed when, in 1992, we considered doing a program on the Earth Summit in Rio. In 1972, the first UN conference on the environment had been held in Stockholm, and *The Nature of Things* had done a program on it. So I got out the show from the archives to screen and was amazed to see well-known experts like Paul Ehrlich and Barbara Ward interviewed as talking heads for three to four minutes each! Today we would never have a talking head for more than twenty or thirty seconds. But what was shocking to me was that I kept thinking, "This is too slow," or even, "Boring." My demand for more information in shorter segments meant that my own intake of information had sped up, and today, watching how young people "multitask" and tweet and watch segments of films and listen to just parts of songs, I see the demand for even faster delivery of more information.

Well, that's a quick run-through of some of my experiences in the media. It never occurred to me that I would become a celebrity. I thought I was merely acting as an agent to transmit information and ideas, but from week to week, viewers don't remember what shows were about or what the details were on each program. I often meet people who say, "Oh, I watched your show last week," and when I ask what it was about, they can't remember. What they do recall is that it was *my* show—that is, they remember me.

When I was doing *Science Magazine,* feminism became a hot topic, and a new show was started called *Some of My Best Friends Are Men.* It got a lot of money and publicity, and I complained to Jim that I didn't see why we never got as much support yet science was so important. Jim's response was prescient: "The important thing is to hang in and stay on air. Series like this come and go, but we're here to stay for the long haul." He was right, and *Some of My Best Friends Are Men* was soon gone, but we kept on air and I was the constant on the series. In hindsight, I see the enormous gift hosting *The Nature of Things* was. Not only did I become a familiar figure after years of hosting the series, I had a platform to present other shows that Jim and I passionately believed in.

seven

FAME AND HEROES

MY DARLINGS,

I wonder if any of you have ever heard of Andy Warhol. He was a famous pop artist in the 1960s and '70s who made huge works of art depicting Marilyn Monroe and Campbell's soup cans, among other subjects. In 1968 he said that "in the future, everyone will be world-famous for 15 minutes." Today, as most of you know far better than I do, postings on Facebook, YouTube, blogs, and other social media can go viral and quickly reach a huge global audience. But what titillates or interests us may disappear from our radar within hours, maybe even minutes.

So what does it mean to be famous? I know some of your friends think your bompa is famous just because I'm on TV, but that kind of fame is fleeting. It's also incredibly superficial, based on one aspect of the person that people choose to focus on. There are people who are famous for being famous, like Paris Hilton, or for having a large derriere, like Kim Kardashian. Simply because I have been on television for years as the host of *The Nature of Things,* I am recognized by people who may know that I am a scientist or an environmentalist. But that person the public sees week after week is not me. Of course, it is my body and my face they see, but the personality that is projected is a creation of the medium—from the words I recite from memory or read from a teleprompter to the clothes I wear and the way I move and the inflection of my voice.

But what does a viewer know about the complex human being I am, with all the good and bad aspects of my personality? Nothing. They don't know that I love being a grandfather or enjoy watching American football, for example. When I stop hosting *The Nature of Things,* I will quickly fade from public memory. Think of the millions of forgotten peasants who made their civilization possible over thousands of years. Like my mother, who was a kind, decent, hardworking human being. We all try to live life as well and as happily as possible, forging relationships with people we care about and share experiences with. But then we will die, and like 99.99 percent of all people who have ever lived, we will pass from memory after a generation or two. You can be elevated onto a pedestal only to be reviled or, even worse, forgotten quickly.

There is a famous video of a statue of dictator Saddam Hussein being pulled down by the people after Americans

had invaded Iraq. I always think of that image as a metaphor for any "famous" person who loses his or her lustre. You
can be raised up, even worshipped, only to be dashed to the
ground, leaving shattered fragments of your previous fame.
The real tragedy is when someone who delights in being
famous fades into obscurity, leaving a washed-up has-been
still yearning to be back in the limelight.

Some continue to do work after their moment in the
public eye. I think of U.S. president Jimmy Carter, who was
much maligned by the right-wing American press after the
OPEC oil embargo in 1973 for turning down the thermostat,
installing solar panels on the roof of the White House, and
wearing sweaters—all to demonstrate the need to reduce
the use of fossil fuels. Ronald Reagan, who defeated Carter,
immediately took down the solar panels and mocked the
notion of energy conservation. Carter, instead of cashing in
on his fame as an American president and seeking finan-
cially rewarding speaking engagements or lucrative board
positions, continued to dedicate his time to working for the
poor, fighting terrorism, and seeking democratic elections.

On December 2, 2014, Jean Béliveau, a famous hockey
player who played on ten Stanley Cup–winning Montreal
teams, died. The outpouring of emotion was far more for
what he did after his hockey career as a consummate gentle-
man in retirement and an ambassador for hockey in Canada.
His fame outlasted his playing career, a rarity these days.

And fame can turn to public dishonour and transform
a distinguished career into disgrace, as in November 2014,

when CBC radio star Jian Ghomeshi was fired for accusations of nonconsensual violence against women, while American comedian Bill Cosby faced renewed accusations that he had drugged and then raped various women.

A long while back, when the WWF—that's the World Wrestling Federation, not World Wildlife Fund—was huge around the planet, its biggest star, once called the most famous Canadian in the world, was Bret "Hitman" Hart from Calgary. He told me a funny story. He had gone on safari to see Africa and was in a jeep with two Africans who recognized him as a famous wrestler. They were watching lions when the jeep got stuck in the sand. The two guides jumped out, jacked the car up, and put boards under the wheels right in front of the lions while Bret sat terrified in the jeep. When they finally got the car out of the sand and onto a road, Bret asked, "Weren't you scared of the lions?" The Africans laughed and said, "Why? You were in the car and we knew you could take care of them!" That's why being famous can be dangerous, because people don't really know you and may have unrealistic expectations of what you can do.

Fame is also dangerous, because when people fawn over you and treat you as if you are special, you can start to feel that you deserve it, that you are better or more important than others, and that you are entitled to be treated that way and to have special privileges.

Famous people can also begin to think they have a right to express opinions as if they are more than mere opinions in public and to expect them to be accepted as truths or special insights simply because they're famous. That's why people get pissed off when a celebrity makes pronouncements about environmental issues like protecting baby seals without understanding the issue or having any reasons for their belief except that baby seals are cute and cuddly.

Television can establish a familiarity between a well-known personality and the viewers that can lead to a false sense of personal connection. After all, people often watch shows in the intimacy of the bedroom, so when they encounter a famous person, they feel an immediate impulse to have a conversation. People often intrude when I'm having a conversation or carrying out an activity with someone else. Once when Severn was an infant, Tara and I took her to a family restaurant in Toronto. After I had given her a bottle, Severn coughed up a bit of milk on her jumper and my shirt. I picked her up and rushed down the street to change our clothes in our car. I set Sev in an infant seat on the car roof as I fumbled for a key to unlock the door. At that moment, someone who apparently had been in the restaurant and followed me out and down the street rushed up and asked for an autograph. "Not right now, please," I pleaded. He walked away in disgust and shouted, "You asshole!"

Nowadays, the biggest intrusion is the cellphone. It seems everyone carries one, and many people approach me asking for a picture. It used to be that a camera was just lifted up, pointed, and clicked, but digital cameras have to be turned on and then the proper program must be found. Most people are not content with a "selfie" and will ask someone passing by to take a picture, which they may do after fumbling with the thing trying to find the right spot to push. Once they have done that, they always do a countdown—3, 2, 1, okay—and then often will decide to get a second shot or will be asked to do so. It all takes a lot longer than film, and if I say "okay" to a request, others jump in and ask for their own personal picture.

I am impressed when someone who is famous uses that celebrity to take informed positions on an issue. For example, I have great respect for Andrew Ference, a professional hockey player who is passionate about protecting the environment and who uses carbon offsets for flying, drives a Prius, and talks to his fellow players about global warming. He uses his recognition as a hockey player to attract people to his ideas, much like you've been doing, Tamo, as an accomplished snowboarder when you have used film footage of boarding stunts to attract kids to your group Beyond Boarding, and once they are caught by your snowboarding shots, you introduce them to environmental issues like the impact of Alberta's tar sands. I like the way you use humour and the fun of trudging up mountains to board down as a way to draw people in.

And I've met famous actors like Leo DiCaprio, Ellen Page, Daryl Hannah, and Ed Begley, Jr., who are informed about the environment and act on their passion to spread the word. In early 2014, I spent a week on the road with the singer Neil Young. Now, I know he is not your generation's great singer—though I hope you recognize some of his songs—but for the boomer generation, he is a megastar. He is also concerned about climate change and built an electric car that is charged by a small engine that burns cooking oil, much like the bus you took on your tar sands tour, Tamo. He decided to drive the car across the United States from Los Angeles to New York, along with his son, who has cerebral palsy like you, Jonathan.

On the way, he decided to make a detour and drive up to Alberta all the way to Fort McMurray to see the tar sands for himself. He was appalled. He had to put a mask on his son because the smell of the fumes from the tar sands was so strong. He was shocked at how the forest and the muskeg were being ripped up and how huge tailings ponds held wastes so toxic that birds landing on them die. He said the devastation was like Hiroshima after the bomb.

Allan Adam, Chief of the Athabasca Chipewyan First Nation, told Neil that their lands were being ripped up and that toxic pollution was spreading into the air and water so that the muskrats and fish the people depended on were either gone or too contaminated to eat. Yet their ancestors had signed treaties guaranteeing that their way of life would be preserved forever in exchange for their land. With the enthusiastic support of the Alberta and Canadian governments, the oil industry has disregarded those guarantees as they have developed the tar sands. Outraged by both the destruction of the land and the abrogation of the treaty, Neil decided to support the Chipewyan First Nation in its pursuit of its treaty rights by taking a four-city tour. If those rights were taken seriously, governments would have to protect the air, water, endangered species, and ecosystems.

"Honour the Treaties" became the theme of the tour, and Neil recruited jazz singer Diana Krall to appear with him in the tour's four cities—Toronto, Winnipeg, Regina, and Calgary—with all proceeds after expenses going to the Athabascan Chipewyan First Nation's legal battle to have its treaty rights recognized and supported. Neil asked me to help, and I suggested that each press conference include a young person to talk about the impact of the tar sands on the future, a First Nations leader, a top-notch scientist, and Neil. All of my recommendations were implemented, and I was asked to join the tour in all four cities.

Neil's fame guaranteed sold-out crowds in every venue, but far more than that, he held a press conference before every concert. Each one was packed with media. I thought of the enormous efforts it took the David Suzuki Foundation, and me, to get media interest in issues. Neil, by virtue of his stardom, brought in a ton of media and got exposure most environmentalists would die for. It reminded me of Paul Watson, founder of the Sea Shepherd Conservation Society, which sends boats out to disrupt whaling operations. At one point, he persuaded Bo Derek, a movie star famed for her spectacular figure in the movie *10*, to attend a press conference to support his organization. One of the reporters demanded to know why Derek was there when she didn't know anything about the issues. Paul replied, "She brought you here, didn't she? That's why she's here."

Well, Neil was far more than bait to lure media, although he did do that. He was impressively informed about the issue. There was huge publicity in each city surrounding his arrival and performance—so much so that the federal government, which had ignored pleas from environmentalists and First Nations, immediately responded to the Toronto press conference, while CAPP (the Canadian Association of Petroleum Producers), like a shill for the oil industry, launched a vigorous counterattack, accusing Neil of being misinformed while ignoring the economic benefits First Nations were receiving directly from tar sands development. But even as Neil was being demonized in the Alberta media, a poll taken in Edmonton, the province's capital city, revealed that 77 percent of respondents agreed with him.

One of the criticisms of Neil was that he was "only" a musician, so why should anyone pay attention to him? Neil batted that off easily, responding that yes, he was a musician, but did that mean he wasn't entitled to have an opinion? "I'm only telling you what I believe," he said. "I'm not telling you what to believe. But in a democracy, everyone should have the right to say what they think and believe."

"You're just using your fame," a reporter exclaimed.

"Of course I am," Neil responded. "Isn't that why you're here?" Shades of Paul Watson.

I am so grateful that Neil was willing to use his fame in such a constructive way and in so doing to take the discussion about the development of the tar sands, climate change, and social justice to a higher level. I'm all for exploitation of fame when that exploitation is based on knowledge and values.

94   An issue related to fame is popularity, which I ached for in high school. When I came out of the camps where my family had been interned for being of Japanese ancestry during World War II, I was extremely shy. As a teenager, I was self-conscious about being Japanese but loved grade 9 at Leamington High School. Many of the students were children of farmers and were bused to school. They were open and friendly, and I got along well with them. I was twelve years old and so was put in a class with the youngest students at the high school.

In the middle of that first year, my family moved to London, Ontario, where my parents felt we would get a better education. I begged to stay in Leamington to complete my year, and so I lived with a Japanese Canadian farmer and finished the year before moving to London.

I arrived in London in time to begin grade 10 and found that friendships and social cliques were already well formed. Besides, I was like a country hick compared with these big-city sophisticates. I felt very much a social "outie," a state exacerbated by the fact that I was a "brain"—I got good grades, which in high school was tantamount to being a leper. I never had the nerve to ask a white girl out, though I dreamed of it all the time. Sadly, there were so few Japanese Canadian families in London that there wasn't much of a pool of potential dates.

Dad had always said if I became a hardened criminal or even a murderer, he would support me in public (but beat the hell out of me in private). Knowing I always had his support was a great comfort and gave me some self-confidence. When an election was being held at school for student president, he urged me to run, even though I didn't want to be humiliated by losing.

"There will always be people better than you," he said, "but how will you ever achieve anything if you don't try? There is no shame in losing, only in not even trying." I got up the nerve to run, and to my astonishment, I won handily.

As student president, I was asked by a reporter for my opinion on something (I can't even remember what the question was). I said I didn't have an opinion. When I told Dad, he was incredulous because he knew I had strong opinions on the subject. "Why didn't you speak up?" he asked. I replied that I knew my position on it would make some people angry or think badly of me. He was disgusted. "David, if you want to be popular with everyone, you will stand for nothing, because no matter what opinion you have, there will always be people who disagree. So if you have ideas and beliefs worth sticking up for—and you'd better have some— then be prepared to be unpopular with some people." That was an important lesson for me.

I know your parents have raised you with a strong sense that you must express your opinions without fear of opposition or disagreement. Tamo, when you got arrested on

Burnaby Mountain for protesting the Kinder Morgan pipeline, Midori and your mother joined you. It's not easy or pleasant when people strongly disagree with you, but I believe democracy is based on our ability to hold on to what we believe and talk about it despite what others think.

In my last year of high school, after I had been elected student president, a newspaper reporter called to ask whether teenagers should be allowed to vote. I replied that I thought most teenagers still lived at home, were more focused on personal relationships than on politics or larger issues, and hadn't had enough life experiences to make informed choices—so I didn't think they were ready to vote. All the student presidents at other high schools had stated that teenagers should be allowed to vote. One said that if teenagers were old enough to be drafted for war, then they should be old enough to vote. Dad was furious that I was the only one saying we were too young.

But when people congratulated him for having such a thoughtful son, and told him that they agreed with me, Dad apologized and said he was proud of me for sticking up for what I believed. I cried when he told me this, but Dad never understood that my tears fell because instead of sticking up for me as he always said he would, he had been embarrassed that I was the odd man out and he changed his mind only when other adults spoke approvingly of what I had done. What other people thought was more important to him than sticking up for me. Even though he had always been a rebel himself, I suppose he could not rid himself of that Japanese desire to fit in. I had believed that Dad was a giant who would never let me down, but now a crack had appeared in the pedestal I had put him on. I guess we call it "growing up" when we realize that our parents are fallible human beings. I lost some of that blind worship I had for him, but I loved him all the more now that I realized he was just a guy trying his best to be a good father.

The kindest, most considerate, most self-sacrificing person I have ever known was my mother—your great-grandmother. My father was the one everyone loved because he was so gregarious. Mom just worked away keeping the family together, doing all the things like shopping, cooking, sewing, washing, and cleaning as well as managing the family's money and accounts and working full-time. She was usually the first up and the last to go to bed. She was the foundation of the family and, to me, the real hero.

Like many Japanese women, she shied away from the spotlight. When people visited, she would rush around making them comfortable, offering tea and cookies and letting Dad be the centre of attention. She was also a wonderful, protective, loving parent but never asked for anything back, no recognition, reward, or even acknowledgment.

When I was about fourteen, I did one of the dumbest, most hurtful things I've ever done in my life. Thinking about it fills me with shame. Mom was in the basement doing the washing, and I was sitting there talking to her. We were talking about money and how hard we all had to work to make ends meet. At one point, Mom said she hoped that when I got older I'd be able to help her and Dad out more. I was feeling sassy and thought I knew everything, and I responded that I didn't ask to be born, so I didn't think that was my responsibility. Then I looked over and saw that Mom was quietly weeping. It makes me cry just writing this down. I was horrified, but I didn't even apologize or try to make Mom feel better. I will carry that memory around until I die. My only hope is that she knew how much I helped her and Dad when they got older, from buying a house in Vancouver so they could retire in it to supporting them until they died. Most important, I hope she knew that I appreciated how hard she had worked, how much I loved her, and how grateful I was to her.

I only really came to appreciate Mom when she began to lose interest in doing the housework, the accounts, and the laundry and began to exhibit the memory loss characteristic of Alzheimer's disease. I didn't believe she had Alzheimer's, because she was always so pleasant and placid; I had assumed that people underwent severe personality change as they slipped into Alzheimer's. After her death, an autopsy confirmed the presence of plaques characteristic of Alzheimer's.

In the years of her dementia, I also came to appreciate my father more. He was a typical Japanese male, the guy out front who was made possible by the hard work performed by my mother. As she lost interest in doing things around the house, he took up the household tasks, which quickly became a burden. Finally I said, "Dad, I can afford it;

you need help. Let's hire someone to give you a hand." I was stunned at his reply: "Your mother gave her life for me, and it's my time to pay her back." And he did. He was with her constantly, caring for her, dressing her, entertaining her.

One evening in 1984, they had gone out for a walk, eaten out, and watched a movie and were walking home arm in arm when Mom dropped to the sidewalk with a massive heart attack. As Dad said, "She had a good death." I came to love my father all the more because of the heroic way he responded to my mother's needs.

The memory of my mother will disappear when my sisters and I and our children pass on. The wonderful human being who was my mother will be remembered for only two generations and then will vanish forever. Why would I, who must constantly struggle to be like her, aspire for any more? And I think of the millions of people who have lived, loved, worked, suffered, celebrated, and, like my mother, vanished from our consciousness in a mere two generations. They were heroic in their humanity, and I can hope for nothing else.

One of the most moving and profound statements about fame and power is from "Ozymandias," by Percy Bysshe Shelley:

> I met a traveller from an antique land
> Who said 'Two vast and trunkless legs of stone
> Stand in the desert. Near them, on the same,
> Half sunk, a shattered visage lies, whose frown
> And wrinkled lip, and sneer of cold command,

Tell that its sculptor well those passions read
Which yet survive, stamped on these lifeless things,
The hand that mocked them and the heart that fed.
And on the pedestal these words appear—
"My name is Ozymandias, king of kings:
Look on my works, ye Mighty, and despair!"
Nothing beside remains. Round the decay
Of that colossal wreck, boundless and bare
The lone and level sands stretch far away.'

Some people do gain fame that is deserved because they are shining examples of what is possible. For me, Mahatma Gandhi, Martin Luther King, Wangari Maathai, Mother Teresa, and Nelson Mandela stand out as people to emulate—even though I know they were profoundly human, with all the foibles and weaknesses of the rest of humanity. But Gandhi and Mandela were special. I am old enough to remember when Gandhi was assassinated, but I was too focused on my own life to have thought very deeply about him. He inspired the people of India to resist British rule nonviolently, and for doing so they were beaten and even slaughtered. But the British couldn't defeat them, and India gained its independence.

Mandela, who died in 2013, stands out as an amazing human being. Please read his remarkable autobiography, *Long Walk to Freedom*. As a result of his beliefs and his actions, he spent twenty-seven years in prison. Twenty-seven years! Can you imagine sacrificing more than a quarter of a century of the best years of your life (that's more than any of you has yet lived), not just locked away in a cell (although that may have been the hardest part), but out doing hard, useless labour, just pounding rocks into dust, and completely isolated from the rest of the world? I cannot imagine surviving such an ordeal with my sanity, let alone with the capacity to embrace those who tormented me, as Mandela did.

On Robben Island, Mandela was forced to dig his own grave then stand in the hole while guards pissed on him. The steady barrage of indignities meant to break his will served only to strengthen him and to turn his ordeal into something positive. He recognized the humanity of his oppressors and realized that if he were freed, to wreak revenge on them would only make him them—an incredible insight but a terribly difficult one to put into action. I know I couldn't. I'd be filled with too much hate and bitterness. I wonder how he kept a lid on anger, the desire for vengeance, and bitterness, whether he suppressed these feelings or actually eliminated them.

But Mandela understood that for South Africa to make a peaceful transition to democracy after the end of apartheid, the white oppressors had to be embraced as fellow citizens of the same country as the newly liberated South African blacks. He elevated the traditional white sport of rugby to a game supported by white and black, an act of pure genius. The crowning moment of his success was being elected president of the government that had so oppressed his people. But in my view, his most incredible act was to limit himself to one term then give way to and support his successors without criticizing them, even when they couldn't live up to his example. It is amazing that a man like Mandela actually lived and succeeded, but what a high bar he set for the rest of us!

To me, heroism doesn't have to be accompanied by recognition and honours. The daily challenge of meeting one's needs, supporting friends, being honest and sharing, standing up for what one believes—this is life, and to do it without compromising one's deepest principles is truly heroic. As you enter the grown-up world, who inspires you? Who are your heroes? You are already mine.

{*eight*}

BIOPHILIA

MY PRECIOUS GRANDCHILDREN,

I am so pleased that your parents all treasure being active—camping and fishing in wild areas. I know how challenging it is to get outside, Jonathan, but your parents have made sure you've canoed and floated down rivers and fished and looked for treasures in forests. But not that long ago people didn't think it was important for us to get outside. It may be hard to believe, but think about how science taught us to focus on one object and ignore everything else around it.

The great strength of modern science has been in concentrating on a part of nature—an ecosystem, a plant or an animal, an organ, a cell, or a molecule. This is called "reductionism," and it is built on the belief that as with a machine, the glimpses we get into the workings of the parts of something can be fitted together to reconstruct the whole.

LETTERS TO MY GRANDCHILDREN

This approach has provided huge insights into the workings of parts of nature—subatomic particles, atoms, genes, and cells.

But we are also recognizing that the sum of all the parts does not yield the whole because new properties called "emergent" result in a whole that can't be predicted from the sum of properties of the parts. The reductionist approach tends to separate organisms from their surroundings—plants can be grown under the controlled conditions of a flask or growth chamber; animals can be reared in a cage or in a yard. But in the real world where they normally exist, plants and animals are subject to variations—seasons, weather and climate, wind, rain, and other organisms. When Jane Goodall set out to study chimpanzees in their natural settings, most of what we knew about them had come from studying the animals in zoos. Goodall observed animals that were totally different from what had been reported—they were highly social, cooperative, and aggressive, used tools, and waged war. One of the reasons I love wildlife artist Robert Bateman's work is that often an animal like an owl or a wolf will make up a small part of a painting devoted mainly to the animal's surroundings. To me, Bateman's work emphasizes that without a recognition of its habitat, we can't truly appreciate a wild animal.

Nonetheless, we tend to see ourselves in a reductionist way. When Nana was diagnosed with heart failure, I was struck by how cardiologists saw her heart in complete isolation from her psychological, physiological, or physical condition. To the heart specialist, the opportunities for treatment consisted of hitting the sick heart with drugs or operating on it. Other things didn't factor into the equa- tion—not the notion that extreme stress (from dealing with her father's illness and death to worry about children and grandchildren); not a physiological imbalance from diet, obesity, or lack of exercise; not environmental conditions.

In the same way, psychologists focus on an individual with little regard to that person's surroundings. Yet stimuli like noise, lights, pollution, or poverty can weigh heavily on a person's psyche. It has been exciting to see that a new approach called "ecopsychology" recognizes how profoundly we are affected and shaped by our surroundings. Now people are realizing that our psychological and physical health both depend on being outside. Study after study shows that recovery from illness or surgery, well-being in old age, performance at work, and children's behaviour are influenced by exposure to nature. To understand why this is so, we have to think about our evolutionary roots.

Our species evolved in the plains of Africa. We weren't covered in fur like other mammals or in feathers like birds, and our nakedness was fine so long as we lived in warm places. Nights could be cold, though, and we had to learn to clothe and shelter ourselves. But basically, like all the other terrestrial mammals, we grazed in open plains, walked through forests, climbed mountains, forded rivers and lakes—we were outside all the time. For 95 percent of human existence, we were nomadic hunter-gatherers carrying all that we owned as we followed animals and plants through the seasons. Our senses of hearing, smelling, and seeing were finely honed for survival out in the open. And that continued after we settled down to become farmers.

The Agricultural Revolution that occurred ten to twelve thousand years ago marked a huge shift in the way we lived. But we still spent most of our time outside, and we were exquisitely aware of weather and climate, as well as other creatures.

In the twentieth century, we underwent a fundamental change in our relationship with the planet. When I was a boy growing up in London, Ontario, my parents, my three sisters, and I lived in a house with about a thousand square feet of living space. It had one bathroom. But I don't ever, ever remember fighting with my sisters about using the bathroom. The constant refrain from my parents was "David, go outside and play." If I pleaded "But Mommy, it's raining outside," I got no sympathy, only "You've got a raincoat. Put it on and call Bobby to play with you." And I did. I remember a puddle as a place of great delight, whether to jump and splash in or to divert through a system of canals and dams. We would toss in chunks of wood or twigs as boats. We had a wonderful trait called imagination, and today's children are no different. I've watched each of you as children, with rooms piled high with plastic gizmos, delight in a simple set of blocks or scrap wood, or build a fort out of pillows on the couch.

What is different is that our houses have steadily gotten bigger to accommodate a decreasing number of occupants but an escalating volume of stuff. Now the average house being built has one bathroom per occupant, I guess because we don't want to have to wait for someone else.

We prefer to keep our children in the house rather than shooing them outside because cars race down the streets and we worry about perverts lurking behind bushes. When I was a kid, we were always outside, but old people often sat on open or covered porches and were our eyes and ears on the lookout for danger. Winters were too cold for perverts to lurk outside in the bushes.

Today the average Canadian child spends only a few minutes a day outside and more than six hours a day in front of a television, computer, or cellphone screen. Even when we are outside, many of us are plugged in via earbuds to some source of sound and blithely unaware of our surroundings.

I was reading J.B. MacKinnon's book *The Once and Future World*, in which he decides that every day for a month he will concentrate on the animals and plants around a small pond. On the very first day, he sees an eagle swoop down and capture a duck and then lose it in a battle with another eagle. While he stands there transfixed by this natural spectacle, people jog or walk by paying no attention to it, not even noticing it.

In big cities, we are focused on each other or the machines we've created, like cars, television sets, computers, and phones. Nature has become alien to us. Even when we go camping, it is often in huge buses towing small cars or motorcycles, complete with a television set and computers, a home away from home. But could we have a physiological as well as a psychic need to be with other species—or "biophilia," as my friend Ed Wilson calls it? Numerous studies are now suggesting just that. Without more exposure to nature, educator Richard Louv suggests, we suffer from "nature deficit disorder," which is expressed as hyperactivity, bullying, or attention deficit disorder. And there is no question that people benefit when animals or plants are brought into hospitals or old age homes.

We need nature in order to be healthy, but we also need to be in nature to observe changes like those in climate.

In a big city, where 85 percent of North Americans now live, it's often possible to go for days without spending time outside. A friend of mine lives in a high-rise apartment in the north end of Toronto. The building is completely air-conditioned. In the morning, he goes down to the basement, gets into his air-conditioned car, and drives down the Don Valley Parkway to his air-conditioned office building, which is connected by tunnels to whole shopping areas. "I don't have to go outside for weeks!" he once told me.

To sense something as subtle as climate change, though, day-to-day differences in weather mean nothing. It takes trends over years to indicate changes in great cycles that affect our lives. Here there is plenty of testimony from people whose lives and livelihood depend on being outside in nature.

Fishers on the west coast of Canada tell us that Humboldt squid, a southern species, are now appearing in abundance in northern oceans. For the first time salmon can be found in arctic rivers. Farmers know they can plant earlier in the year and harrow the fields for winter later. Hunters tell stories of bears that once would have been hibernating wandering about in the winter because temperatures are so warm that they wake up, and birders record earlier arrival of birds on their way north and later departure to the south.

Years ago, I asked Matthew Coon Come, Grand Chief of the Quebec Cree, whether he noticed any changes in climate, and he told me that by September, beavers are usually in a frantic level of activity preparing their dens for winter. "Now," he went on, "in October, they're lying around drinking martinis and smoking cigars as if they've got lots of time." He was joking, of course, but he was telling me the animals know winter is coming later in the year. Inuit people have been warning us for years that winter ice is thinner, that the properties of spring ice are changing, that there's more open water earlier and it lasts longer than in the past.

Ski resort operators and professional skiers tell us that seasons are shorter and so resorts are moving lifts higher up mountains. Meets in Europe are being cancelled for lack of snow. Canadian hockey icon Wayne Gretzky's childhood is well known—he developed and honed his skills each winter on a backyard rink his father, Walter, built each year. Today there's no such opportunity for a young Gretzky because the temperature is too warm to make a rink where he grew up.

Foresters know that an insect the size of a grain of rice, the mountain pine beetle, has been kept under control for millennia by five or six days of temperatures below −30°C every winter. But with rising global temperatures, mountain pine beetle populations have exploded in British Columbia, transforming pine forests from green to the red of dead leaves, a loss of billions of dollars' worth of trees. The insurance industry was one of the first private-sector areas to warn that climate change is real and that its consequences are rising costs from weather-related problems (hurricanes, tornadoes, forest fires, floods, drought).

Mayors of oceanside villages tell us that higher tides and storm surges are destroying wharves and seawalls at costs that are crippling for small communities. The most sought-after oceanfront properties are now threatened by the encroachment of rising waters. In Calgary and Toronto in 2014, extreme floods caused tens of millions in property damage, while water experts warn of faltering water levels in lakes and dams. When I was in Kuala Lumpur recently, I casually asked the taxi driver on the way to the airport whether he noted any change in climate in Malaysia and was surprised by his animated response. "In the past," he said, "summer temperatures might reach 33 or 34°C three or four days. But now, the temperature is that high for weeks or even more than a month!" I had thought the tropical areas were warming more slowly than northern and temperate regions, although I remember attending an Intergovernmental Panel on Climate Change (IPCC) meeting in the 1990s at which a Kenyan farmer told me he had always decided when to plant and harvest his fields based on the sequence in which wild plants appeared but they were now coming up at different times, thus messing up his decisions. These are all anecdotal stories from people who are not climate scientists or experts. They have no axe to grind or vested interest in fossil fuels, but they depend on nature's cycles and regularities for their survival and well-being.

Today much of our food is packaged, and we buy it with little evidence remaining of blood, fur, scales, or feathers of animals or inedible roots, stems, and leaves of plants. So we forget or fail to recognize that every bit of the food we eat for our nutrition was once alive. I remember the ten-year-old son of a CBC producer laughing at his sister because "she thinks Kentucky Fried chicken is a bird!" What keeps the planet habitable and healthy for animals like us are the "services" performed by nature—pollination of flowering plants, decay of vegetation and meat, capture of energy from the sun by plants to fuel all life, filtration of water as it percolates through the soil, exchange of carbon dioxide for oxygen.

I once appeared on a program in Vancouver with the Vietnamese Buddhist monk Thích Nhất Hạnh. When we met, he suggested that before we begin a conversation we take a walk outside. I have to admit, I had been anxious to meet and talk to him and was annoyed at his suggestion. I was in a hurry. He was accompanied by a group of monks who trailed after us as we walked in silence around the large grounds beside the building we were meeting in. Soon I began to think about my breath and then reflected on all the green leaves around us. We can't see air, so we seldom think about it, but as we slowly ambled along, I began to sense the air being refreshed by photosynthesis, the plants sucking in carbon-laden air from my every breath and exhaling oxygen in return. By the time we had circled the field, I was completely absorbed in thoughts of gratitude to the rest of nature for the air we depend upon. As we prepared to enter the building, Nhất Hạnh remarked, "Wasn't that refreshing? And we didn't have to spend a cent!"

That little walk powerfully reminded me that nature is our touchstone. However sophisticated and technologically advanced we may be, we are biological creatures, utterly dependent on her beneficence for clean air, water, and food. But we will only value and fight to protect what we know and love. I know how much each of you has valued nature as you grew up, from dinosaurs to rocks and frogs and creeks. That's why you will all be warriors for things that matter.

nine

THE STATE OF THE WORLD

MY DEAR GRANDCHILDREN,

You are living in a unique and critical period in the history of Earth. Human beings have grown so powerful that we have become a new kind of force on the planet. We are shaping its physical, chemical, and biological properties on a geological scale. That's why scientists now refer to this as the Anthropocene epoch, or the Age of Man—the period in Earth's history when *we* are the major factor affecting its properties.

Although we have powerful technologies to explore every nook and cranny of the planet in search of resources and opportunity, and a global economy that makes use of what is found, we know so little about the interconnectedness of everything on Earth that we can't anticipate the consequences of all we do. So we often end up undermining the very things that keep us alive—air, water, soil, and biodiversity. The disastrous effects of our actions are appearing very suddenly, so it is urgent that we act to curb our negative impact on the biosphere.

114

I have long maintained that one of our species' unique attributes is foresight, the ability to use our acquired knowledge and experience to look ahead, anticipate opportunities and hazards, and then deliberately choose a path to minimize danger and maximize benefits. Although I'm an atheist, I have read parts of the Bible and learned its lessons, and I find it interesting that some of the stories in it reinforce the importance of foresight.

One of them is the story of Joseph, whose jealous siblings pushed him into slavery at the hands of the Egyptians. Because Joseph could interpret dreams, he came to the attention of the pharaoh, or king. Joseph foresaw years of famine and recommended that the pharaoh prepare for it by storing grain. The pharaoh took his advice, and Egypt survived seven years of drought and famine because of Joseph's ability to see the future.

Another biblical character, Noah, a carpenter, was instructed by God to build an immense ark and place plants and animals in it two by two. Rains and flood came, and Noah, his family, and the plants and animals survived because he had prepared in anticipation of what was to come.

These stories, whether mythical or not, reinforce the importance of looking ahead and planning accordingly. Today, scientists, engineers, and supercomputers have given us an amplified ability to look ahead; and for decades, they have been warning that the collective impact of human activity is threatening the survival of our species. The most recent study, which came out as this book was being completed, is an urgent call to change our ways because human beings are passing planetary boundaries.[1] Your parents are my children, so they know and will have taught you about the global ecological problems we are facing, from deforestation and toxic pollution to climate change and the acidification of the ocean.

At the heart of the crisis is the rapid degradation of the very source of our lives and livelihood—namely, nature itself. I'm often asked by people why it's so important to protect wilderness when most Canadians live in big cities. That people even ask that question reveals a world so shattered that in the city we can't see how our lives depend on nature.

TWO EMINENT ECOLOGISTS have spoken about the dangers of the loss of nature for decades, and I have been honoured to know and be considered a friend and colleague by both of them. In 1968 Stanford professor Paul Ehrlich, a butterfly expert, wrote *The Population Bomb,* a bestseller that warned of the catastrophic impact of exploding human numbers on nature. The book created a sensation, and also controversy. Ehrlich proposed an all-out effort to stabilize population using family planning, contraception, and abortion, the last of which—abortion—riled the right-to-life advocates. He also suggested that food sent to developing countries might be laced with sterilizing compounds, a recommendation that raised accusations of racism and genocide. Even the environmental community has been reluctant to tackle overpopulation for fear of being labelled racist or invoking genocide against certain groups.

Our effect on the biosphere is not just a matter of how many of us there are. Our consumption habits also have an impact, because everything that we consume, from food and clothes to cars and energy, comes from the earth and goes back to it when we are done with it. When per capita consumption is calculated for a population, we can see that we in the industrialized world are "overpopulated" in our use of resources and generation of waste. But the economies of industrialized countries are tied directly to consumption; the more people, the more growth there is in the economy. Consumption is an integral part of the economies of the industrialized countries, so those countries do not want to address hyperconsumption among the wealthy nations. That's why at the Earth Summit in Rio in 1992, instead of addressing the issues of consumption and population directly, delegates simply dropped them from the agenda.

Another famous ecologist, Edward O. Wilson of Harvard, has expressed his great concern about habitat destruction and species extinction. He grew up in the southern United States, where he wandered the swamps and forests and fell in love with nature. But when he was a boy, he caught a fish that pierced his eye with a spine on its fin, ultimately damaging his vision. So he decided it was better to study smaller animals that could be examined close up, and he became a world expert on ants.

Wilson's great gift, aside from his writing skills, was his ability to see the big picture, extrapolating from his work to higher levels of complexity. Wilson has tried to show how little we know about life's diversity by estimating the number of species on Earth. He freely admits that we haven't a clue how many there really are, but he has made crude estimates by looking at the total number of species of plants and animals that have been identified. If we assume that the proportional representation of different groups among identified species reflects a similar proportion throughout life on Earth, then estimates can be made about how many there might be. We probably know most species of big plants and animals, but if we add ones that might live in difficult places for us to explore, like the deep ocean, boiling vents, beneath the polar ice, and far underground, there may be 10 million species of animals and plants. If we add the estimated number of bacteria, fungi, and other microorganisms, the number comes to 100 million possible species.

One of the early attempts to make an estimate was that of Terry Erwin in 1983,[2] when he was working for the Smithsonian Institution. He laid plastic sheets on the floor of a stretch of Panamanian forest, then sent a fog of pesticide into the forest canopy. Insects rained down, and when Erwin examined them, he found that most were unknown to science. In one species of tree, he found 160 beetles that appeared to be adapted to that specific tree species. Since beetles make up about two-fifths of insects, he calculates that there are four hundred species of insects specialized to that species of tree. Since there are estimated to be fifty thousand species of tropical trees, then, extrapolating from his study, Erwin suggests that the total number of species in the world is grossly underestimated: there may be 30 million species. We simply don't know, but it is acknowledged that the identified species are a fraction of the total number that exist, and as habitat is destroyed by clear-cut logging, burning, and flooding, species we don't even know about are being lost.

Among animals, the most recent number of known vertebrate species is:

mammals—5,487
birds—9,990
reptiles—8,734
amphibians—6,515
fish—31,153

In contrast, the number of identified insect species is more than a million.[3]

Scouring the literature, Wilson calculated that about 1.5 million species have actually been identified—that is, given a name. Being named, however, merely means that someone in a lab has classified or "keyed out" the species in the taxonomic system by following along a series of branches in traits such as kinds of organs, colour, and shape until distinct characteristics of that species have been reached. But that does not indicate that anything is known about that species' basic biology, like its geographic distribution, its population size, how it interacts with other species, what it eats, how it reproduces, or where it lives. So even though we may have identified close to 2 million species, we know next to nothing about the web of living things on Earth; yet we claim to be able to "manage" forests, air, water, and species like salmon and halibut, grizzlies, wolves, and caribou. It's absurd.

Of 40,168 known species, scientists in the International Union for Conservation of Nature estimate that extinction threatens one in four mammalian species, one in eight birds, one in three amphibians and conifers, half of all reptiles and insects, and 73 percent of flowering plants. That represents a rate of extinction thought to be a thousand to ten thousand times the normal extinction rate (one species for every million species a year). It would mean that between 2.7 and 270 species disappear every day!

We have entered another major extinction episode, the sixth in the past 439 million years. The first five involved the sudden (in a geological sense) loss of 50 to 95 percent of all species in the fossil record, including the last episode, 65 million years ago, when the dinosaurs disappeared. The current extinction wave differs from the others in that human beings are causing it, not geology—through habitat destruction or degradation, agriculture, overexploitation, and the introduction of invasive species. Species diversity has recovered after past spasms of species loss, but recovery takes about 10 million years. We think of dinosaurs as losers because they suddenly went extinct, but they flourished for more than 150 million years before disappearing. We've been around as a species for only 150,000 years!

In October 2014, the World Wildlife Fund released the 2014 *Living Planet Report,* which concludes that between 1970 and 2010, 52 percent of animals among known vertebrate species had disappeared.[4] This is a catastrophic decline in Earth's richness and tears holes in the web of diversity that keeps the planet habitable for animals like us. Our concern is no longer just about protecting the charismatic or cute and cuddly animals and trees. Although large animals like rhinos, tigers, whales, and pandas are endangered, it is the loss of the collective role that the disappearing plants and animals play within the biosphere that is of greatest concern. Their loss threatens survival of animals at the top of the food chain—animals like us.

What we do or do not do in the coming years to address issues of climate change, habitat destruction and species extinction, overexploitation of resources, toxic pollution, invasive species, and ocean degradation will have little impact on the lives of elders like me, who are in our last years. But what is or is not done will reverberate through your entire lives. You have everything at stake, yet little power to affect decisions being made at the political and corporate levels.

IT'S IMPERATIVE THAT we recognize how much the world has been altered in a short time. When I was born, in 1936, the world held about 2.2 billion people, already a huge number for any species; but within my lifetime, that number has more than tripled. Every addition to the human population has to be fed, clothed, and sheltered, and that increases the amount of air, water, and land needed by our species (our ecological footprint), and it reverberates through the rest of nature. That's what Paul Ehrlich warned about in 1968, when the world population was half what it is now.

We were living in Leamington, close to the American border, when I was about eleven and Dad took us to visit the Detroit Zoo. It had a huge impact on me. I was dumbstruck by the beauty and diversity of animals on display, and that inspired me to want to become a scientist to study them.

Fifty years later, in the 1990s, when she was about ten or eleven, I took Severn to the Toronto Zoo. Remembering my experience at the Detroit Zoo, I expected her to show the excitement and joy that I had felt when I was a child. How the world has changed! At each exhibit, Severn's first question was "Are there many of these left, Daddy?" As a child, she was already aware of extinction, and it was uppermost in her child's mind.

When I was a boy, Dad and I often drove through the countryside looking for new places to fish, and the car windshield would be spattered with insects. We'd have to stop every so often and wipe the window clean. Insects were abundant, and I took up a hobby of collecting them and pinning them in display boxes. Mom made me a net from cheesecloth, and Dad made a wire hoop to string the net onto and then secured it to a handle. I now had an insect net. Most people love the colour and splendour of butterflies, but I found beetles far more interesting because they had such an amazing profusion of sizes and shapes. This was underscored by a comment by one of the great geneticists and evolutionary biologists, Britain's J.B.S. Haldane. He was a devout atheist who is said to have remarked, "The Creator, if He exists, has an inordinate fondness for beetles."

Not surprisingly, my children—your parents—share a passion for catching and eating fish and looking at insects. As they were growing up, I bought nets, killing bottles, pins, and display cases, but to my disappointment, the children refused to kill any insects for display. My children were happy to catch them, observe them in bottles, even film them, but insisted on releasing them back where we found them. And so that's been the attitude each of you has held too.

Many young people today have such a different attitude to nature than mine was because they are aware of the changes to the planet. When Severn was about nine, I took her with me to northern British Columbia, near Alaska, to film the delta of the K'tsim-a-deen Valley, where grizzly bears came to feed in the spring. Environmentalists wanted to protect the area against logging and development. We went to the valley in a large sailboat and after we had finished filming headed back to Prince Rupert. Sev was down in the cabin of the boat when I spotted a killer whale. "Sev, come up quick! There's a killer whale!" I yelled. She rushed up in time to see the animal close to the boat, and then it dove. We anxiously scanned the horizon waiting for it to come back up for air. The minutes ticked by, and then it emerged again. "There it is!" I shouted, pointing with excitement. When I didn't hear Severn responding excitedly, I looked down to find her weeping. "What's the matter, sweetheart?" I asked. "Look how far it went on one breath of air!" she wailed. "And they're kept in such small pools at the aquarium!" She was a child, yet she was aware of how wrong it was to confine such a magnificent animal that had evolved to roam over vast distances.

When we lived in Leamington in the 1940s, there was a massive hatch of mayflies off the waters of Lake Erie every spring. I thought of them as "flying gonads" because as adults, their sole goal was to find a partner, mate, lay eggs, and die. There were so many mayflies that they would coat houses so that you couldn't see inside; they would cover highways, causing cars to skid and crash; and their carcasses would pile up on beaches a metre thick as fish gorged on the flies laying their eggs on the water. But as farmers increased their use of pesticides, these toxic compounds were carried into the lakes as runoff from the fields. In only a few years, the mayfly population had plummeted to almost nothing. The ecological impact of the loss of that biomass must have been huge as birds, fish, frogs, and bats all lost a major source of food.

Years later, I was on the train coming back home from my first year of college in New England, and as we travelled high above the Niagara River, I looked down the gorge and could see people with rods casting and pulling in twisting silvery fish with every cast. When I got home to London, I told Dad about it, and we drove to the river the next day to find that silver bass were migrating up the river to spawn. It was an incredible biomass, a huge population of fish, and we caught many that day. But within a few years, pesticide runoff from farmers' fields and pollution from chemical dumps like the Love Canal had poisoned the waters and severely reduced the number of silver bass—another casualty of our thoughtless use of the environment as a toxic dump.

It's important to remember the world as it was in the childhood of elders so that we have reference points against which to compare today's world. UBC's world-renowned fish biologist Daniel Pauly—with whom Sarika got her master's degree—coined the phrase "shifting baselines" to describe the phenomenon that over time, in the absence of input from elders, people forget what once was and readily accept the current or recent state of the world as if it's the way it always was. And as we spend less and less time outside, we become less aware of change and don't care if things *do* change.

The complexity and abundance of life in the world are being diminished by human demands. The human population has exploded, and the United Nations predicts that it will total 10 billion by 2050. That means, as of this writing, an additional 3 billion mouths to feed and bodies to clothe and shelter, and a huge addition to our ecological footprint.

Our impact on Earth has been amplified many times by technological advances that allow us to explore and extract resources from every part of the planet, from ocean depths to mountaintops, from deep within the earth and across deserts. In the ocean, fish hardly have a chance against huge factory ships that can stay at sea for weeks, freezing catches brought in by longlines that are miles long with thousands of hooks, or nets big and strong enough to hold several 747 jets, dragged along the ocean floor between two boats. Navigation and communication technologies used in the process include radar, GPS, sonar, cellphones, and computers. But we don't think about that when we buy fish.

Consider the dozens of ingredients in a pizza, car, or cellphone. From spices like pepper to rare earth metals, rubber, and lithium, components of the things we all buy and use come from around the world, but we are unaware that purchasing them has global repercussions. When activists lead campaigns (for example, against Nike for exploitation of workers in poor countries), recommend sustainable seafood or lumber, or support fair trade with the growers of coffee, consumers do learn and respond, but this happens for tiny fractions of the products now whizzing from every part of the globe.

Add together the collective global impact of population, consumption, the global economy, and technology, and it is clear how we have become a geological force. Human activity has so disrupted processes on the planet with consequences that what were once called "acts of god" or "natural disasters" now carry the undeniable imprint of our species. We have become almost like gods as we affect natural events such as weather and climate, earthquakes, floods, drought, mega-fires, hurricanes, and tornadoes. Once, our fear of gods acted to restrain human excesses, but now we have ourselves become the gods.

126

We should pay far greater attention to ourselves—our actions, motives, and consequences—but we have become so impressed with how clever and inventive we are that we think this is all progress and that we can carry on as we do. However, we are too ignorant about how the world works to anticipate the consequences of our new technologies. That's why I have broken from most of my colleagues in genetics who feel that GMOs (genetically modified organisms) are a boon to humankind. I believe that there are enormous potential benefits to them but also that our knowledge of how genes act within a genome is still so primitive and incomplete that there will be unintended and deleterious consequences of our manipulation, and that therefore we should rein in our impulse to exploit GMOs, as well as every other new insight or invention, as quickly as possible. That's an economically driven imperative, not a thoughtful goal. We should always remember that technologies widely heralded as wonderful innovations, from nuclear power to DDT and CFCs to pharmaceutical drugs, have often failed to live up to the hype or been found years later to have unantici-pated consequences. We need a different way of assessing the long-term consequences of new technologies when they are invented and a greater sense of humility in the face of our ignorance.

A general principle governing the way we deal with toxic waste seems to be "out of sight, out of mind." So we have disposed of some of the most potent toxins—nerve gases— by dumping them into deep ocean trenches, and we seem unconcerned that the encasing canisters will corrode there over time. Now it is proposed to entomb long-lived nuclear waste in mines deep in the earth for hundreds of thousands of years, forgetting that even the pyramids are only a few thousand years old and are wearing away. Nothing humans have created has resisted breakdown and corrosion over thousands of years.

If CO_2 is pumped into depleted wells, more oil can be recovered while the CO_2 remains in the ground. So the industry proposes to remove CO_2 from emissions and pump it underground, a technique called carbon capture and storage (CCS). Now that the fossil fuel industry is being forced to confront the need to reduce carbon emissions, the government has poured billions into this technology. This assumption that CCS will be the answer sometime in the future allows the companies to continue pumping oil out of the ground and us to burn it without reducing greenhouse gas emissions—in other words, business as usual. But we don't know why the CO_2 doesn't come back out, and we know almost nothing about life underground and what effects the acidification of CO_2 and the etching of limestone caps will have. We are simply happy to believe that putting massive amounts of CO_2 out of sight is a solution.

Energy powers modern society, and we have built our way of life around fossil fuels. But as with nuclear power, problems are created by the end products: radioactive waste and greenhouse gas. "Peak oil"—the point when humans will have used half of all oil deposits—was predicted decades ago, and the spectre of declining availability spurred further exploration in extreme environments, deeper water, farther underground, in the Arctic. Environmentalists embraced peak oil as the threat that would drive innovation and a shift away from fossil fuels, but to our shock, new deposits continued to be found, and then hydraulic fracturing (fracking) exploded as a source of "natural" gas and oil.

Fracking—like chemical pesticides that kill all insects just to eliminate the one or two pests—has to be one of the dumbest, most shortsighted, and most dangerous practices. Fracked gas is released by pumping massive amounts of water and sand containing dozens of chemicals, including known carcinogens, under high pressure into wells deep underground, causing shale to shatter and release bubbles of gas and oil that were trapped in the rock. It is astounding that there is so much oil and gas trapped this way, but suddenly the explosive growth of fracking in the United States has supposedly created a "glut" of energy. I can't see how there can be a glut of any nonrenewable resource—only a seeming abundance that is temporary. The gas released is methane, a greenhouse gas that is twenty-two times as potent as CO_2, and Americans are finding a high rate of leakage that more than offsets the claims that fracked gas is a "transition" to renewable fuels because of its lower climate change footprint than coal or oil. As should be obvious, oil and gas from a fracked well will deplete rapidly, thereby requiring more and deeper wells for an ever-diminishing return. Water pumped into the wells is contaminated and can flow into underground aquifers, while the intense concentration of high-pressure wells is inducing seismic activity, including earthquakes. Fracking clearly indicates the lack of concern for consequences both immediate and long term.

People often ask, "What is the most critical problem we face? Is it climate change, toxic pollution, overpopulation, deforestation, ocean degradation, species extinction?" My answer is that these are all critical issues, and there are more. We don't know which one may be the issue that will do us in, though right now climate change looms as our existential challenge. I firmly believe that habitat destruction and species extinction will greatly diminish the chances that our own species will survive even if we do manage to get greenhouse gas emissions under control.

To me, the real challenge is the human mind, which is driving our actions: our beliefs and values shape the way we see the world, which in turn determines how we will treat it. So long as we assume that we are the centre of the universe and everything revolves around us, we will not be able to see the dangers we create. To see those, we have to recognize that our very lives and our well-being depend on the richness of nature.

The wired world we thrive in today, with personal electronic devices that give us access to the world's information and to the rest of the world's population, shatters everything into tiny snippets in which the exquisite interconnectivity of all becomes invisible. Throughout human existence, the search for causal relationships has been vital. What caused that storm? Why did he get sick? Where did the animals go?— these crucial questions were often answered by "the gods" or other superstitions. But in asking the questions, we could also be led down a path to understanding. Today, there are many crucial issues whose causal basis leads to solutions— Why are fish in Banff National Park contaminated by Russian pesticides? Where are the immense piles of plastic in the oceans coming from? What causes autism?—but in our electronic world, these connections are often invisible. Things happen, but we seldom ask anymore why or how.

Even when we do carry out environmental assessments, they are done for individual projects, such as a well for fracking or a clear-cut patch, but ignore the collective impact of many such developments together.

We base many of our projects on the assumption that continued "progress" in technology will help minimize or eliminate the negative "costs" of development. So, for example, although the science clearly indicates that we have to radically reduce the output of greenhouse gases to avoid catastrophic climate change, rather than reducing fossil fuel use and moving toward a clean renewable energy future, we invest in unproven ideas like carbon capture and storage on the assumption that it will work and therefore we can carry on without changing our actions. Moreover, since technological innovation is assumed, the cost of climate change for future generations, who will bear the brunt of those costs, is discounted. Do not be assured by these assumptions.

What will the world be like when all of you reach adulthood? I have spent much of my life thinking about that and dreading the possibility that the events I've been warning about may come to pass. In 1988–89, when I was preparing for the radio series *It's a Matter of Survival,* I interviewed more than 140 scientists and experts from around the world, and by telescoping all their input into a few months, I could see that the biosphere was under assault. I thought of the world as a basketball covered in ants that were eating away its surface. The accelerating decline in biodiversity on Earth results from the continuing destruction of habitat that is now referred to as "ecocide."

There have been all kinds of scientific reports on the state of the planet, on air, water, soil, biodiversity, oceans— all depressingly similar. Human beings have become so numerous and demanding that we are causing the continued decline in the life-support systems of Earth. Climate change has suddenly exploded as a very real threat to the survival of our species, and what happens in the next decade could well determine our fate. Even if we were, by some miracle, to work together and switch off fossil fuels to clean renewable energy, biodiversity will already have been drastically diminished.

132   How can people bring children into a world when the future is so uncertain? There have been other moments in history when the future must have seemed equally bleak—when human numbers were reduced to catastrophically few as during great epidemics like the "plague" in Europe, the North and South American epidemics of smallpox and other European diseases that wiped out entire populations of indigenous people, and the Holocaust in Europe. This moment differs in that it is the entire biosphere, on which *all* life depends, that is being transformed. But your parents, by virtue of having you, have made a big commitment to work hard for your future.

I am a big fan of George Monbiot, a columnist for the *Guardian.* In October 2014, he wrote a very moving *cri de coeur,* a cry from the heart, in response to a report that 52 percent of animals in known vertebrate species had disappeared in the previous forty years:

> Who believes that a social and economic system which has this effect is a healthy one? Who, contemplating this loss, could call it progress?[5]

But our current extinction of animals is not a new phenomenon. Humankind has had a long history of extinguishing species, beginning with the big, slow-moving ones that provided a lot of meat and could be outwitted by an ape like us, armed with a nimble brain and simple tools like stone axes, clubs, and spears. Monbiot adds:

> The loss of much of the African megafauna—sabretooths and false sabretooths, giant hyaenas and amphicyonids (bear dogs), several species of elephant—coincided with the switch towards meat eating by hominims (ancestral humans)... As we spread into other continents, their megafauna almost immediately collapsed.

In fact, Monbiot suggests that the sudden disappearance of big animals may be the best indication of the arrival of humans to an area. According to him, even ecosystems regarded as untouched wilderness have already been modified by our species:

> The habitats we see as pristine—the Amazon rainforest or coral reefs for example—are in fact almost empty: they have lost most of the great beasts that used to inhabit them, which drove crucial natural processes.
>
> Since then we have worked our way down the foodchain, rubbing out smaller predators, medium-sized herbivores, and now, through both habitat destruction and hunting, wildlife across all classes and positions in the foodweb.

But why have we become such a hyperdestructive animal? Three obvious factors are rapid population growth, because every additional person needs water, food, and shelter; the explosive growth of powerful new technologies, which amplify our ability to travel and to detect and exploit more of Earth's species and habitat; and a hyper demand for consumer goods, all of which come from Earth and go back to it when we are finished with them. Monbiot reaches a bleak conclusion about the consequences of the industrialized way of life:

> In a society bombarded by advertising and driven by the growth imperative, pleasure is reduced to hedonism and hedonism is reduced to consumption. We use consumption as a cure for boredom, to fill the void that an affectless, grasping, atomised culture creates, to brighten the grey world we have created.

When I was a boy, my Depression-scarred parents urged us to purchase necessities, but you only have to go to a big box store like Walmart to see that we have moved far beyond buying what we need. Instead, we indulge ourselves in the purchase of useless gadgets and items that are meaningless and ultimately without value. Monbiot takes this into account too:

> The extraction of the raw materials required to produce them, the pollution commissioned in their manufacturing, the infrastructure and noise and burning of fuel needed to transport them are trashing a natural world

infinitely more fascinating and intricate than the stuff we produce. The loss of wildlife is a loss of wonder and enchantment, of the magic with which the living world infects our lives.

We are constantly harangued about the necessity of maintaining growth in the economy, but growth is simply a description of a system. Growth cannot be an end; it can only be a means to something. Why do we aspire to endless growth? And in a world in which even nature is finite, not limitless, steady growth forever is impossible. Studies indicate that the growth that does occur benefits primarily the already obscenely wealthy: the richest 1 percent of Americans reap 93 percent of the benefits of growth, namely, more purchasing power for frivolous things—houses, boats and planes, fashionable clothing, automobiles, anything to flaunt that wealth. Workers, in contrast, labour at boring jobs, work longer hours, and are burdened with more stressful demands. Yet there seems to be little alternative to the current economic system, which has been so tightly embraced by politicians and corporate executives alike.

In Monbiot's words again,

Thus the Great Global Polishing proceeds, wearing down the knap of the Earth, rubbing out all that is distinctive and peculiar, in human culture as well as nature, reducing us to replaceable automata within a homogenous global workforce, inexorably transforming the riches of the natural world into a featureless monoculture...Is this not the point at which we challenge the inevitability of endless growth on a finite planet? If not now, when?

I can't imagine a more urgent moment for a fundamental shift in the way we see our place within the biosphere. To carry on as we have is suicidal and a terrible denial of our unique attribute of foresight. Naomi Klein's book *This Changes Everything* raises climate change as the crisis of our time and points to capitalism itself as the cause of our inability to stem our destructive path. I agree. How can we shift the paradigm?

Yet Monbiot's bleak words offer us an insight that provides real hope. The triad of issues—population, technology, and consumption—unlike the issues of habitat loss, ocean depletion, and climate change, are tractable because they are human issues. We may think we know enough to manage the planet, but we don't. That is a human conceit. The challenge is us, and we are capable of changing; we can strongly influence the way we behave; we can learn and develop. With greater humility, with understanding of the exquisite interconnectivity and interdependence of everything on Earth, we can relearn to value nature and rediscover our place within this world.

{*ten*}

BARRIERS TO CHANGE

Until one is committed, there is hesitancy, the chance
to draw back ... The moment one definitely commits oneself,
then Providence moves too ... A whole stream of events
issues from the decision, raising in one's favor all manner of
unforeseen incidents and meetings and material assistance,
which no man could have dreamed would have come his way ...
Whatever you can do, or dream you can do, begin it.
Boldness has genius, power, and magic in it!

W.H. MURRAY, quoting Goethe

MY LOVELY ONES,

You are living through a moment unprecedented in all of human existence. The sudden confluence of explosive growth in human numbers, technological dexterity, and consumptive demand is having a huge impact on the properties of the planet itself. Some of the consequences include an alteration in the biological and chemical composition of the atmosphere, water, and soil and massive geophysical change in terrestrial and aquatic ecosystems. It means that you are heading toward huge changes in weather and climate as well as in the biological productivity of forests, reefs, wetlands, and prairies. The scientific warnings of our potential fate have been issued with increasing urgency over decades, but there has been reluctance to meet the challenge on the scale that is needed. The question is why.

Some reasons are obvious. For one thing, unless faced with an immediate crisis on the order of Pearl Harbor or Fukushima, politicians are extremely risk averse; they don't want to make commitments that will involve a huge out-lay of money or will take many years to complete, though recent history is full of examples of governments jumping into hostilities that consume them for years. For another thing, a corporation's highest priority is to maximize profit as quickly as possible. To bring about real change, we have to see that the real world—the one that sustains us, that lies beyond politics and economics—is nature, and that the barriers to action are psychological. I love and agree with Murray's plea that one must make a commitment in confronting a crisis, but that is the hardest thing to do because we all see the world through beliefs and values that are powerfully influenced by politics and economics.

In our struggles to solve problems—like shifting from clear-cut logging to ecosystem-based management, reducing greenhouse gases by moving to renewable energy, or calculating the value of the ecosystem services of nature before building dams or opening a new subdivision, impos- ing regulations and a tax on market transactions, or moving toward a no-net-growth economy—the most difficult challenge is to overcome the mind-set that does not believe that something is possible or that fears that if that thing is instituted, it will be incredibly destructive. As Al Gore pointed out in his film *An Inconvenient Truth,* the Chinese character for "crisis" is made up of two parts: one meaning "danger" and the other, "opportunity." This is a profound insight—that a moment of great threat becomes a chance to commit to a different path, to do things differently and avoid exacerbation or repetition of the dangerous situation. Einstein famously defined insanity as "doing the same thing over and over again expecting a different result."

A crisis provides the chance to get it right. In 2008, the world experienced an economic meltdown after big banks made easy loans to people who could not repay on the faulty assumption that property value would rise forever. When the property buyers defaulted and banks could no longer cover the money paid out, we had a fantastic opportunity to get things right by reining in the banks and their greedy CEOs. Instead, U.S. president George W. Bush, and then President Barack Obama, somehow found hundreds of billions of dollars to give to the banks simply to get them back up and running again—a perfect example of that definition of insanity. Meanwhile, proponents of renewable energy have to beg for crumbs. Think of what could be done if the trillions committed to bailing out banks were committed instead to moving us onto a different path!

Over and over again, when confronted with dangers from our current practices in energy, forestry, mining, pharmaceuticals, and more, we fail to find different ways of approaching the problem. If the use of fossil fuels contributes to climate change, the fossil fuel industry should see its mandate as providing energy, not fossil fuels, and find new sources that do not create greenhouse gases; if clear-cut logging is destructive and unsustainable, the forest industry should look to an ecosystem-based way of harvesting trees and thereby maintaining the integrity of the forests while enabling logging to continue; and so on. But the mind of executives is usually set too strongly to countenance radical change, even when the health of the entire biosphere and your futures are at stake, as they are with climate change.

In 1973, during the Arab–Israeli war, OPEC (Organization of the Petroleum-Exporting Countries), a consortium of mostly Arab states, decided to put pressure on the West by decreasing the amount of oil sent to Western countries. Gas prices skyrocketed, and oil shortages led to long lineups at gas stations. There was real panic as industrialized countries realized how vulnerable they were in their dependence on oil from the Middle East. (As I write this, the power of OPEC is again in view as member nations and the United States have created a glut that has sent prices crashing.)

In response to that crisis, Canada set up a committee

under the eminent scientist Ursula Franklin to study how the country should respond to the threat posed by OPEC. In 1977, Franklin completed her report, *Canada as a Conserver Society,* which recommended that we use our resources much more efficiently, conserve them by reducing waste, and move into renewable energy, such as wind, which would provide an opportunity for Canada to become a world leader in a new area. It was a prescient piece of work, and just think of what could have happened had we made a commitment to those goals! Canada could have been a world leader in an area that is exploding today. Instead, the report was accepted, put on the shelf, and soon forgotten. We reverted to the old ways as soon as the oil flowed again.

Denmark was equally alarmed by the OPEC embargo, but its response was to seek alternative energy sources, most notably, wind. Engineers had scoffed at the notion that windmills could contribute significant amounts of energy, pontificating that it was impossible to produce more than 2 percent of a country's energy needs with wind. Like the "experts" who pronounced it impossible for machines to fly, those early engineers were expressing limits imposed by their own mind-set, not those set by nature. Denmark made a commitment to reduce dependence on oil and now aims to produce close to half of its electricity from wind.

Over and over, we are told that solutions to problems are "impossible," usually on the basis of economic cost, but seldom because of real scientific or engineering barriers, and almost always because the blocks are in our minds. Laws

142

of nature do limit what is possible, of course. From physics, for example, we know we can't build a spaceship that will travel faster than the speed of light, an antigravity machine on Earth, or a perpetual motion machine. Laws of chemistry involving atomic properties and rates of diffusion and reaction dictate the chemical reactions that can be carried out and the kinds of molecules that might be synthesized. And in biology, all species are constrained by their ecosystems' carrying capacity (the maximum number of a plant or animal species that can be supported indefinitely by a habitat or ecosystem), the species' energy needs, and their metabolic requirements for air, water, and food. Our species' ability to adapt to many different ecosystems does not remove us from the constraints of carrying capacity, because it is the biosphere that ultimately imposes limits on sustainable populations.

But other things are not fixed and can be changed. Borders delineating human political boundaries, governments, capitalism, the economy, corporations, markets, and currency—these are not forces of nature; they are human constructs and so can be modified and regulated to conform to the boundaries dictated by nature. But we react and respond to those global factors by acting as if our creations somehow are inviolable and must be maintained, so we try to shoehorn nature into our priorities and make her conform to our needs.

For years, the David Suzuki Foundation and I have opposed salmon farms, not because we are against fish

farming but because we are against how it's done and what
is farmed. There are three strong reasons for opposing the
salmon farms in British Columbia. First, the fish are grown
in open net pens. That means that feces and food pellets
fall through the mesh and pollute the ocean, while diseases
such as infectious salmon anemia (ISA), infectious hema-
topoietic necrosis (IHN), furunculosis, and bacterial kidney
disease, as well as parasites like sea lice, can explode in the
cramped nets and spread to infect wild fish in the vicinity.

Second, salmon are carnivores and so have to be fed
pellets made of perfectly edible fish. Other than alligators,
terrestrial carnivores aren't farmed for meat. That would be
like raising tigers for their meat by feeding them chickens,
pigs, or goats. It wouldn't make sense, but carnivorous fish
seem to be acceptable as farm animals. The salmon will eat
pellets containing plants, but when the amount of plants
reaches a certain level, the salmon flesh is considered unap-
petizing for human consumption. In other words, we can't
convert a carnivore into a herbivore and still want to eat it.

Third, most of the salmon grown in Pacific farms are
an Atlantic species. Unlike all of the Pacific salmon species
(except for steelheads), Atlantic salmon are repeat spawners,
meaning that unlike the Pacific salmon, they don't die after
spawning. Instead they lay their eggs, go back out to sea, and
come back again, perhaps as many as three or four times. So
they are tough. I once filmed salmon caught in a net that
had been put into Lake Ontario. It was a mix of Pacific (coho,
chinook) and Atlantic salmon. All of the Pacific fish were

dead, but every one of the Atlantics was still alive and kicking. If there are already five species of salmon spawning on the west coast, why on earth deliberately introduce another species with the risk that the fish will escape and outcompete the Pacific salmon? They escape from farms by the thousands every year, but the Department of Fisheries and Oceans has long argued that Atlantic salmon do not reproduce in Pacific rivers. That's because DFO once deliberately tried to introduce Atlantic salmon in the Pacific by dumping thousands of them into those waters. The fish never managed to spawn successfully, so DFO has repeatedly stated that they simply cannot make it in the Pacific. Then biologist John Volpe found that not only were Atlantic salmon successfully spawning in the Pacific, but two-year-old salmon were being caught at sea. Even though DFO is mandated to protect the wild species, it has never moved to ban raising millions of an alien species.

The solution to all three objections is obvious. First, put the animals in hard containers, either in the water or on land. After years of arguing that that would be too expensive, the salmon-farm industry is being shown that it can be done on land by a First Nations community on Vancouver Island and another operation in the state of Washington.

Second, if carnivores must be raised, then clearly feeding them fish that are caught in other waters is not sustainable. In fact, not only is fish meal fed to salmon and other farmed fish species like cod, it is also a food supplement for chickens. So demand is growing while the population of fish used in the feed is decreasing, and the rapidly rising price of fishmeal reflects that. For years, I proposed that if we must raise salmon, then insects might be a viable alternative feed, something that Brad Marchant, a businessman and entrepreneur, seized on. Today, his company, Enterra, uses waste food, which the city of Vancouver pays him to take, and feeds it to an insect called the soldier fly. Eighty percent of the food waste is water, which evaporates, while the food that goes through the larval digestive tracts comes out as high-grade fertilizer and the larvae provide high-quality feed for fish and chicken alike.

Third, all rearing of Atlantic salmon in Pacific waters should stop, period. Although solutions to each of the problems exist, the mind-set that justifies continuation of the old ways remains the biggest challenge to implementing what must be done.

For years, environmentalists fought the forestry practices of clear-cut logging. If you've ever seen a large clear-cut, you know you don't have to be a forester to feel in the pit of your gut that it's simply wrong. James Gosnell was one of the great Nisga'a chiefs, a brilliant orator and ferocious fighter for his people. He once told me about his first encounter with a clear-cut forest. He had been walking along a familiar trail when suddenly he came out onto an opening. He said he couldn't breathe because he felt the earth "had been skinned." How could anyone treat a forest that way? he wondered. Forest companies argued that to be globally competitive, they had to use clear-cutting; it was too expensive to cut selectively.

To forestry companies, a forest is simply "fibre" (for paper) or lumber, not a complex community of organisms. They treat the forest as an agricultural field, in which all uneconomic species are considered "weed" species. (One of these weeds was yew trees, until they were found to possess a potent anti-cancer compound.) All the debris from clear-cut logging (called "slash") is collected and burned, then small trees are planted, like so many vegetables. Insecticides are sprayed, fertilizer is spread, and herbicides are often used, all to raise a "crop" of trees. These destructive practices are rationalized by the mind-set that a forest can be simplified into useful tree species. But the forest and all the ecosystem services the intact ecosystem performs are ignored and thus lost.

And so it goes. When cars were first devised, all manner of options emerged—steam-driven cars, electric cars, gas-powered cars... Because gas is portable, packed with energy, and cheap, the internal combustion engine took over. Some modifications were made, but still they burned fossil fuel. GM's ill-fated electric car was a grand experiment that fell victim to a mind-set that simply wouldn't accept it as a viable alternative. Today, electric vehicles promise to be the future of automobiles, but it has taken decades to reach this point and resistance is still high.

The auto industry prides itself on its creativity and ingenuity, but it should be ashamed of the flimsy excuses it raised against higher emission standards, seat belts, and mileage targets. The same criticism applies to the fossil fuel companies. Refusing to acknowledge that their game is energy, they cling to the notion that fossil fuels are so deeply embedded in our way of life that no other form of energy is realistic.

We boast of our intelligence, and yet the most abundant form of energy, available everywhere on the planet and acknowledged, even worshipped, by cultures of the past, is sunlight. What an opportunity for every human-created surface—buildings, roads, vehicles, clothes—to harvest this form of energy! No need for oil wells in deep waters, distant jungles, or arctic settings; no need for extreme sources like tar sands and shale; no need for transport by long pipelines, ships, trains, or trucks. And no more health costs from emissions after burning or during extraction. All it takes is a mind shift, a look at the problem through other lenses.

But industries are quick to promise that they can find solutions while keeping on the same old path. It's strange that when industries assure us how wonderful they are, we pay so little heed to their track records. They tell us how marvellous their technology is and how they will use world-class techniques to avoid spills, but if spills happen, don't worry—they will clean it all up. Really? Twenty years after the *Exxon Valdez* oil spill, you just have to turn over a rock in Prince William Sound to find traces of that oil. And in the biggest spill ever, BP's offshore explosion in the Gulf of Mexico, the "solution" to the escaping oil was not capturing it but burning it on the surface of the sea or spreading massive amounts of toxic detergent to break up the slicks so it could sink out of sight. It is mindboggling to think that fossil fuel companies have any credibility worth listening to when they make their submissions about how safe their activity is and how dependable they are now and will be in the future.

Would you believe that nuclear energy was once touted as so cheap it wasn't worth monitoring how much you use? Today we know that nuclear energy is the most expensive form of energy there is. We have no solution for how to handle waste, yet after the experiences of Chernobyl and Fukushima, nuclear energy is still put forth as a solution to climate change.

We are told over and over that engineers design these systems to be "foolproof." Tell that to the people at Fukushima or Chernobyl. And what about Three Mile Island?

Besides, what is a foolproof technology? It's a system "free of fools." Yet who among us hasn't been a fool at some time in our lives? We catch a cold but come to work anyway because we can't afford to lose a paycheck. We go to a party and drink way too much, so when we go to work, we're still hungover. We fall in love and lose fifty IQ points. All kinds of circumstances cause us to act foolishly. The only foolproof technology, as HAL, the computer in the movie *2001: A Space Odyssey*, recognized, is one in which humans are removed from the equation.

There have to be other ways of doing things that do not involve putting whole ecosystems or even the entire biosphere at risk. The most important thing to do is recognize that we cannot continue as we have, that we have to take a different path. Instead of rationalizing, justifying, raising phony objections, lying, we need corporations and governments to change their mind-sets and to make the commitment to change their actions. Once the commitment is made, as Murray says, new avenues open up.

Have you ever seen films of penguins, on the edge of the ice, about to leap into the ocean but afraid to because of carnivorous leopard seals waiting for them? I feel we are like that with issues like climate change. The penguins hesitate, diddle around. Finally, one of them takes the plunge, and then all the others follow, because together their risk of being caught and eaten is reduced. The one that is first takes the biggest risk but also has first crack at whatever the group is going after.

Let me end this letter with one final story. I was beginning my last year of college in 1957 when an epidemic of Asian flu hit campus. I caught it and staggered to the infirmary to check in. (A funny thing was all the other guys in the infirmary with the flu hissed at me because I was Asian. Good-naturedly, of course.) I lay there in bed so sick that all I could do was listen to the radio. Suddenly, on October 4, I was electrified to hear that the Soviet Union had launched a satellite into space. It was sensational. I hadn't even known there was a space program.

This was during the Cold War, and the Soviets were frightening, as they were taking over governments in Africa and South America. For the Americans, every hour and a half, the beep-beep of *Sputnik* was a reminder of Soviet technological might. As the United States ramped up its space program, recruiting seven "astronauts" with great fanfare, the Soviets piled up one space first after another: the first animal, a dog, Laika; the first man, Yuri Gagarin; the first team of cosmonauts; the first woman, Valentina Tereshkova. It was clear that the USSR was very advanced in science, engineering, and medicine.

Americans didn't shrink from the challenge, moan about the Soviets' great lead, or object to the cost of catching up. Instead they threw themselves into the challenge—forming NASA (the National Aeronautics and Space Association) in 1958, pouring money into science departments in universities, supporting students in science. It was a glorious time even for a foreign student like me. We just had to indicate an interest in science, and all kinds of opportunities opened up. On May 25, 1961, President John F. Kennedy announced a plan to get an American astronaut safely to the moon and back before the end of the decade, thus beating the USSR in a space race. It was an audacious goal, since it was far from clear how or whether the nation could do it. But they made the commitment to try, and on July 20, 1969, American astronaut Neil Armstrong set foot on the moon, the first human landing there.

It was an astounding achievement, because it was accomplished in less than a decade and because the United States was the first—and so far the only—country to land people on the moon. But even more impressive are all the unexpected benefits of the space race. Since 1976, NASA has published *Spinoff,* listing hundreds of technologies that have resulted from space efforts, ranging from laptop computers and GPS to twenty-four-hour news networks to freeze-dried food, space blankets, cordless vacuums, cochlear implants, and ear thermometers. And Americans still feature prominently every year when Nobel Prize winners are announced—all because in 1957, the United States made the commitment to catch up to and pass the Soviet Union in space. I tell my American friends, "It's un-American to say 'meeting the challenge of climate change is too great' or 'will cost too much.' That's not the American way. The America I knew and admire would seize on this opportunity and commit to solving it in the knowledge that enormous unpredictable benefits will fall out along the way." The most important thing in meeting any challenge is, as Murray said, to make the commitment.

So here we are, my dears. My generation and the boomers who followed have partied as if there is no tomorrow. We didn't see that we were leaving you a world depleted of diversity and opportunity and heavy with impending eco-logical crises. Given the enormous growth in the scientific community and the tools it has to assess the state of the world, we, uniquely among all animals, have the potential to act on our foresight. We know we can affect the future by what we do today. But we have all kinds of cultural and social blinders, such as religion and economics, that make it difficult to recognize the hazards we face.

Youth today are relatively uninvolved in politics, and that's understandable; without an ability to vote, young people cannot directly affect an election outcome. But you have everything at stake in what is or is not done by politicians today. I believe that the warriors on behalf of your future have to be parents and grandparents. That's our job—that's what we commit to when we have children. Parents have to make your future a political issue and demand that politicians act to move along a different path. History informs us that the most important step is to make the commitment to change, to move toward a different future, one that will be richer in opportunity and that will inflict fewer challenges on you and your children. Once a commitment is made, as W.H. Murray says, "all manner of unforeseen incidents and meetings and material assistance" will pop out, and the important thing is, he says, quoting Goethe, to "begin it."

eleven

GRASSROOTS CHANGE

MY DARLING GRANDCHILDREN,

Tamo and Midori, I am so proud of the activist commitment you've made to the Tahltan people to help in their fight to protect their land in the Sacred Headwaters of northern British Columbia. You both are ready to step up and put yourselves on the line for issues. Jonathan, the needs of disabled people in society are something that you have encountered all your life, and I hope you will speak up about your rights and needs as you take your place in society with other disabled people. And, Ganhi and Tiis, the role of First Nations in our society continues to evolve, and I know you will be ready to fight for your just place in Canada. Ryo, my latest grandson, welcome to the world. I can only imagine what state the world will be in and what kinds of issues you will face when you are older, but I hope you will be as engaged as your parents and your cousins have been. It's so important for us all to try to make this a better place for all people.

People often come up to me and say, "Thank you for the work you are doing," as if my public visibility on different issues somehow relieves them of being actively involved themselves. Many people have supported the David Suzuki Foundation because they like what I am doing, but if I ask someone what *they* are going to do about it, a typical response is "You're on television, so you have a big influence, but what difference does it make what *I* do? I'm a drop in the bucket." I've been lucky to have had a platform, *The Nature of Things*, that has enabled me to present important issues to the public. But I'm still just one person too, a drop in that bucket. If we recruit a lot of drops, however, we can fill any bucket there is.

This is what a grassroots movement is. I don't believe a grassroots movement depends on one person, no matter how inspirational or charismatic that person might be. He or she can motivate people, galvanize action, and influence behaviour or beliefs, but no one is indispensable; nor should they try to be. Many others preceded them, and although the civil rights movements in the United States and South Africa would have taken a different and perhaps longer course had there been no King or Mandela, I believe that others could have made a significant contribution also. So thank goodness, no one is indispensable.

In the end, few people can hope to achieve what Mahatma Gandhi, Martin Luther King, Wangari Maathai (Nobel Peace

Prize winner and originator of the Green Belt Movement in Africa), or Nelson Mandela did. But we can all be a part of something that can grow into a movement. What matters most is that we *try*. I've been on the losing side of a lot of issues, but I don't think I've wasted my time; it's the striving for positive change that matters. If we don't try, how can we ever achieve change for the better? I hope that when my life is coming to an end, I will be able to look each of you in the eye and tell you that I have loved you with my entire being and that I tried to do the best I could for you. My greatest joy would be for you to know I tried to make this a better world for you. It is so important for you to act on what you believe.

Many people who try to make a difference do fail, for many reasons, and many succeed without fanfare or broad recognition. I'm thinking about Tara, your nana, who was active all through your lives. She worked not just on environmental matters but on educational issues. When Severn and Sarika were in elementary school, Nana worked hard on a committee that replaced the concrete on the school playgrounds with grass and wild plants, built planter boxes and installed them around the schoolyard, planted a vegetable garden and fruit and nut trees on the school grounds, created a butterfly garden, and installed birdhouses. And I'm sure you know of other people who volunteer, who become activists on issues like feeding the poor or raising money for victims of genocide, hurricanes, earthquakes, fires, and so on around the world. To me, these people are the heart of any grassroots movement: people who work to help others and to make a positive difference in their communities. People with passion that burns within them, with a vision to aim for and a willingness to devote time and energy and money to support it. They do it selflessly without worry about recognition or awards, and you know what? The rewards are in the satisfaction of acting on their beliefs and the joy of working with others who share the same goals.

Over the years, I've tried to get a movement started by travelling across the country on speaking tours. My inspiration was Terry Fox, the young man who in the 1980s lost his leg to cancer and set out to run across Canada to raise awareness of the disease. When he dipped his leg into the Atlantic at the start, it was with almost no press, but as he hopped across the Maritimes into Quebec, the media began to pay attention. By the time he arrived in Toronto, public interest was huge. Hobbling from there up the vast distance to northern Ontario, he was suddenly stricken with a return of the cancer that had taken his leg. I remember watching on television as he tearfully announced he was abandoning his run but vowed to return to complete it. I am sure most people, like me, cried as he said these words and then wailed when he died a few short weeks later. He became a Canadian legend, and annual runs in his memory have raised hundreds of millions of dollars for cancer research. He made a massive contribution. But long before Terry, in the Freedom Rides of 1964, college students (most of them white) rode buses into Mississippi to persuade black people to register to vote. The violent response of Mississippians, the courage of the students and their black supporters, and the ultimate response of the federal government led to huge changes throughout the South as black people were registered to 157 vote and changed the political landscape.

I have never had hopes of duplicating Terry's success or that of the Freedom Rides, but I hoped I might help trigger something that would grow far beyond me. So I agreed to travel to every city with a CPAWS (Canadian Parks and Wilderness Society) office to drum up more public interest in supporting parks across the country. I travelled to five cities across Canada with examples of green technologies (including a Prius, which wasn't yet available in North America) to showcase the opportunities for developing new industries. I visited six cities across Canada with the Nature Challenge: Human Element tour in 2002, an attempt to get people to take concrete steps to reduce their ecological footprint and to spend more time outside in nature. And in 2007 I did a major bus tour, called If You Were Prime Minister, through more than twenty-four communities from St. John's, Newfoundland, on the east coast to Vancouver on the west coast, trying to motivate people to urge the prime minister to act on climate change.

Each attempt was a lesson. We learned that it's not good enough just to give an inspiring speech; there has to be an "ask," a concrete request to do something. And after the tour ends, people who have responded have to be "fed"—supported with some money, ideas, and suggestions—in order to maintain their enthusiasm. The initial enthusiasm quickly gives way to the daily demands of living and so requires constant reinforcement.

In 2004, two former environmental activists, Michael Shellenberger and Ted Nordhaus, presented a paper called "The Death of Environmentalism: Global Warming Politics in a Post-environmental World."[1] It hit like a bomb and served a very useful role in making activists rethink what they were doing.

I had come to a similar conclusion on my own, because many "victories" we had celebrated years before had come back to haunt us. For example, Alaskans were enjoying rich economic returns because of vast oil deposits and were anxious to drill for oil in new areas. One of those areas was the Arctic National Wildlife Refuge (ANWR), which is the calving grounds of the Porcupine caribou herd. The Gwitchin people depend on that herd for their culture and well-being, so Norma Kassi, a Gwitchin leader, asked me to help them protect the herd. I made a film for *The Nature of Things* about the herd and the fight to keep drilling out of ANWR.

In one of the segments, we filmed at the Sierra Club in Washington, DC, where activists gathered because a "rider" enabling drilling in ANWR had been attached to a piece of other legislation. One of the peculiar quirks in American politics is that a bill to, say, improve education might include a rider enabling bicyclists to ride on the sidewalk (I made this up to show that a rider doesn't have to have anything to do with the bill). The idea is that legislators will want to pass the education bill, and the rider about bicycling will automatically be passed along with it. At the Sierra Club, the activists filed into a room filled with telephones and began to call senators across the country to pressure them to vote to defeat the bill. It was an amazing strategy of hardball politics. When the vote was to be taken, everyone gathered to watch the results on television. One by one, the senators stood up to vote. Everyone cheered when those who had been wavering voted against the bill, and a huge yell went up when the bill was defeated. It was an exhilarating exercise and the results were gratifying, but I couldn't help feeling uncomfortable because this was just hardball politics in its toughest form. The politicians who defeated the bill did not understand the deep reasons the rider was bad, and there was little movement toward an enlightened government. So, sure enough, years later pressure again built up to drill in ANWR, and I made another film about the caribou herd. The bill was defeated again, but a Republican-dominated Congress promises to continue to press for drilling in ANWR unless the spiritual and ecological value of the herd and the threat of drilling are acknowledged and understood by all—or until a bill is passed and wells are drilled.

Thirty to thirty-five years ago, environmentalists celebrated many victories. I had supported west coast First Nations in Canada who opposed a proposal to drill for oil in the treacherous waters of Hecate Strait, a shallow waterway rich in fish between the mainland and the islands of Haida Gwaii. We stopped it. We prevented oil supertankers from Alaska from travelling through BC coastal waters,

160

and stopped dams at Altamira, Brazil, and at site C on the Peace River in British Columbia. But three decades later, just as with the issue of the Porcupine herd and ANWR, we are fighting the very same battles again. These battles are symptoms of deep, underlying assumptions and values that haven't changed. Our victories failed to change the way we see ourselves in the world.

That's why, in the fall of 2014, I began my last cross-Canada bus trip, called the Blue Dot Tour. The tour got its name from an essay by Carl Sagan, an astronomer who was a fantastic communicator in the media. In 1990, a space probe, *Voyager 1,* approached the edge of our solar system, six billion kilometres from Earth. Sagan asked NASA to turn the satellite's camera around to take a picture of Earth. The resulting picture showed a backdrop of black with dots of light, which are distant stars. And taking up 0.12 of a pixel was a pale blue dot that was Earth, a mere speck in the vastness of space! That prompted Sagan to write *Pale Blue Dot: A Vision of the Human Future in Space,* including these lines:

> Look again at that dot. That's here. That's home. That's us. On it everyone you love, everyone you know, everyone you ever heard of, every human being who ever was, lived out their lives... The Earth is a very small stage in a vast cosmic arena. Think of the endless cruelties visited by the inhabitants of one corner of this pixel on the scarcely distinguishable inhabitants of some other corner, how frequent their misunderstandings, how eager they are to

kill one another, how fervent their hatreds. Think of the rivers of blood spilled by all those generals and emperors so that, in glory and triumph, they could become the momentary masters of a fraction of a dot.

Our posturings, our imagined self-importance, the delusion that we have some privileged position in the Universe, are challenged by this... The Earth is the only world known so far to harbour life. There is nowhere else, at least in the near future, to which our species could migrate... the Earth is where we make our stand... There is perhaps no better demonstration of the folly of human conceits than this distant image of our tiny world. To me, it underscores our responsibility to deal more kindly with one another, and to preserve and cherish the pale blue dot, the only home we've ever known.[2]

I feel so fortunate to have known Carl; I met him when he was a guest on a series I created and hosted called *Interface: Science and Society*. Way back in the 1970s and '80s, there was a very famous late-night talk show host named Johnny Carson, who had an interest in astronomy. Carl was a professor at Cornell University who had written a book called *Cosmos*, which had sold a few copies but was not a bestseller. Johnny had either heard about it or read it, and he invited Carl to be on his show. Carl was like no scientist who had ever appeared before on American TV—good-looking, bright, articulate, and passionate about science, with a terrific sense of humour. It was a dynamite combination, and he was an instant hit: his book skyrocketed into bestseller status, and he was invited repeatedly to be on Carson's show. He went on to write and host the series *Cosmos* for PBS, and by PBS standards, it was a blockbuster. Sadly, Carl died when he was still relatively young.

As he implied in his essay, our planet is an insignificant speck of dust in the cosmos; yet within that thin membrane of air, water, and land we call the biosphere, all of life and human history has taken place. From space, we see the fundamental oneness of the planet—air, water, and land are all interconnected, and no boundaries or borders are visible. For this reason, we chose the title of Sagan's essay as the title of our tour.

The Haida have seen our world this way for millennia. During the 1970s and '80s, the Haida fought against the practices of the forest industry, which for years had clear-cut vast swaths of forest, leaving the thin soil exposed to desiccation by the sun and erosion by rain. It took millennia of change and adaptation for those forests to evolve to what they were, and once they were cut down, it would take many centuries to recover anything like the productivity that they once had. Creeks and streams that once supported salmon runs were choked with debris from logging that took place right to the water's edge.

In 1985, the Haida drew a line across a logging road above Windy Bay on Lyell Island, determined to stop the loggers and logging trucks from entering the area. They succeeded and eventually negotiated the creation of Gwaii Hanaas National Park Reserve, which covers almost 1,500 square kilometres. It was a stunning achievement, the protection of a vast area not just for the Haida but for all Canadians.

But that wasn't enough. The Haida continued to press for an extension of the park boundaries into the water, contending that the land, air, and water are part of a single system. Try to imagine "managing" salmon only in the ocean or only once they entered rivers—it's absurd. In 2010, the Haida were successful, and the boundaries of the park were extended ten kilometres out to the sea floor. Even then, the boundary was a human construct; nevertheless, it recognized the interconnectedness of land and ocean.

A good friend of the David Suzuki Foundation, environmental lawyer David Boyd, wrote a book analyzing the environmental commitments of countries around the world and noted that 110 nations include some kind of environmental commitments in their constitutions.[3] But not Canada. He proposed that the Foundation press for a constitutional amendment to enshrine the right to a healthy environment. I was electrified by the idea because it seemed to offer a way to get out of the battles over specific issues. Recognizing that our health and well-being depend on clean air, clean water, clean soil and food, clean energy from photosynthesis, and biodiversity would form the foundation for the way we would live. Now logging companies, mining companies, and other such entities would have to show whether or not an activity harmed the environment—the responsibility would no longer fall on the people who would be affected by the activities.

164

That's why I decided to take one last stab at bringing about change by getting back onto a bus. People at the Foundation developed a program to make sure that the excitement we generated around the idea would carry on after the bus had gone by. They did this using the work of Harvard's Marshall Ganz, who said that social movements could be created based on three factors: motivation, knowledge, and learning.

The idea is that people go into a community and recruit a highly motivated person who believes in the cause, is well informed, and is willing to work flat out to raise money, recruit support, and so on. That person finds six other people who are also highly motivated and willing to commit their time. The first person is responsible for those six, who report to him or her. Each of those six recruits six more and is responsible for them. Every person involved is only responsible for shepherding six people. This technique has proved to be very powerful; U.S. president Barack Obama used it to raise support and huge amounts of money and, as we know, was successfully elected twice.

In his last campaign, one of the critical states Obama had to win was Florida. Michiah Prull, an American who had come to the University of British Columbia for his education, was hired to work for the Foundation but was then recruited by the Obama team to go to Florida to head the outreach campaign there. The campaign was highly successful, and he was thinking of moving to Washington, DC, after Obama won again, but Peter Robinson, the CEO of the David Suzuki Foundation, offered him a position, which he accepted. At twenty-five, Michiah, already a seasoned campaigner, headed up the Blue Dot Tour.

The basic idea of the tour was to ignite a movement to eventually get a constitutional amendment in which the right to a healthy environment was guaranteed by Canada's Charter of Rights and Freedoms. The strategy was to focus first on getting local municipalities to adopt a declaration of a right to a healthy environment and local legislation to ensure it. As this was building, we would try to get support and eventually legislation at the provincial level. To make a change in the constitution, Canadian law requires support of seven provinces that include at least 50 percent of the nation's population, so provinces that support an effort will themselves champion other provinces to work for the federal change in the constitution.

It is a big idea that has only been successful once in the past, but I loved the approach as it was developed by the Foundation. Will we succeed? I have no idea, but I wouldn't have bothered if I didn't think it could be done. Regardless, the discussion that will ensue will be a huge opportunity to ask what really matters to us as a country. Once we ask what a healthy environment would mean, we have to say clean air; clean water; clean soil and food; photosynthesis, which provides all the energy in our bodies; and biodiversity, which is the source of these critical elements.

The Blue Dot team also began to recruit performers to participate at our events so that we could appeal to a wider audience than just committed enviros. Earlier in the year I had accompanied Neil Young on the Honour the Treaties tour, which championed the First Nations of Fort Chipewyan, who were suffering from the downstream effects of the Alberta tar sands. Neil had packed houses for his performances and raised a million and a half for the Fort Chipewyan First Nations. I got to see firsthand how celebrity brings media, huge adoring crowds, and, especially in Alberta, apoplectic criticism. Some of the questions were "You're just a musician—what do you know about the issues?" "You're riding around in a big polluting bus. Aren't you a hypocrite?" "Is it true that you fly around in private jets?" Watching Neil let the criticisms roll off his back was a great learning experience for me. His most pointed answer was "I'm not saying what should happen to the tar sands. I'm just asking Canada to live up to the promises that were made in the treaties with the First Nations."

When Neil agreed to play for the Blue Dot Tour, we jumped with joy, first, because he's a terrific performer, and second, because we knew that he would draw not only a large crowd but other performers as well. From that point on, as we let it be known he was coming, excitement began to build. Jim Cuddy, lead singer of the popular Canadian band Blue Rodeo, had indicated he wanted to support us even before Neil had agreed. Fred Penner, the much-loved children's singer, offered to perform, as did Bruce Cockburn,

Feist, Barenaked Ladies, the folk-rock band Whitehorse, Inuit throat singer Tanya Tagaq, the legendary Québécois singer Gilles Vigneault, and many more. Wow, what a lineup!

We wanted to emphasize that this tour wasn't about an "environmental" issue but about how we will live together on this planet. Issues of social justice, hunger and poverty, gender equity, security, genocide, war, and terror are all relevant to a sustainable future. So we were delighted when writers Silver Donald Cameron and Margaret Atwood, human rights activist Stephen Lewis, spoken-word poet Shane Koyczan, artist Robert Bateman, doctor and underwater expert Joe MacInnis, First Nations leader Ovide Mercredi, and the Royal Winnipeg Ballet agreed to take part.

Ovide, a past head of the Assembly of First Nations, jumped on board to support us because, as he said, what the Blue Dot Tour was aiming for was a central part of what most First Nations sought in negotiations for their treaty rights. Many had been promised their traditional practices such as trapping, hunting, and fishing for "as long as the wind blows, the rivers flow, and the grass grows."

I wrote to First Nations leaders in every community we would visit on the tour, explaining our goals and asking to meet with them so that I could thank them for what all indigenous people had taught me. That's why we made a long trip to Miawpukek (Conne River), a Mi'kmaq community in Newfoundland, on the first leg of our tour. Along the way, we met with Mohawks in Quebec, Six Nations peoples in Ontario, and Cree on the prairies. We ended on the Musqueam Reserve in the city of Vancouver. As we travelled, we collected vials of water in each community so that we could combine them all and pour the water into the Fraser River as a ritual.

We were suggesting adoption of a Declaration for a Healthy Environment that, alongside grand words about the importance of air, water, soil, and biodiversity for our survival and well-being, contained a commitment to pass legislation protecting those elements within two years. It was our hope that perhaps five or six months after the tour ended, we might get the first community to adopt the Declaration. But DSFer Sophika Kostyniuk had done the preparatory work well, and as our tour began in Newfoundland, we heard that a subcommittee of the city council of Richmond had considered the declaration and unanimously agreed to submit it to the full council.

Then, two weeks after our tour had begun, we heard that Sophika and a teenager had made statements supporting the Declaration. The boy, Gavin Li, had been born in China and gave a moving talk about how he had never experienced air so clear you could see the stars, or water so clean it could be drunk without worry, until he came to Canada. He urged that these things be recognized and protected. People were moved to tears, and the council passed the Declaration unanimously. Our tour wasn't half over and we already had a positive result. And more followed. I met Denis Coderre, newly elected mayor of Montreal, and urged him to make Montreal the first large city to pass it, and he agreed to try. He succeeded in getting it passed, but not before Vancouver did.

Most inspirational was a story of a small town (population 5,500) called The Pas, in northern Manitoba. A grade 6 teacher spotted the Blue Dot website and watched the video we had prepared for the tour. She was intrigued and showed it to her students, who called the mayor to come watch the video. He came to the class, watched it, and urged the kids to come to a city council meeting and suggest adoption of the declaration. They did and were so persuasive that the council unanimously adopted it, becoming the second municipality to do so. One ten-year-old boy who attended the Blue Dot event in Victoria was so inspired that he wrote to all of the city's councillors urging them to adopt the declaration, which they did unanimously. As of March 3, 2015, twenty-five municipal councils have adopted it, including Yellowknife, a resource-dependent northern city.

The Blue Dot Tour ended at the Musqueam Reserve on November 10, 2014. By the end of that year, more than 11,500 people, representing more than half of Canada's municipalities, had registered to become spokespeople in their communities for the right to a healthy environment. This is what a grassroots movement should be: action from the bottom up. As I say to people, "We elect people to *serve* us; they are our *servants,* and it's up to us to tell them what we want them to do."

The challenge is still great. We have to keep people excited and engaged as we press for more and more communities to come on board, and as they do, we will begin to discuss the need for provincial adoption of the declaration.

Even if the declaration does flounder, the discussion of the idea is important. Too often, environmental issues are constrained by the need to ensure that their cost is not too much for the economy to support. But the demand to keep the economy growing is itself unsustainable, and a healthy environment, which we depend on for our lives, and indeed for all of life, should take precedence over economic and political considerations.

Tamo, you already are deeply involved in grassroots activity, so you know very well what the challenges are in mobilizing support at that level, but you also know how individually empowering it can be. It was so great that you happened to be in Prince George, in northern British Columbia, when we came through and you could contribute your personal experiences and priorities. You were awesome, and now your sister, Midori, is part of your activity. Soon, I know, you will be joined by your cousins; after all, Ganhi is already five! And all of you have far more at stake in these issues than old guys like me. This is about the kind of world you will grow up in, and I believe at the grassroots level, people know this and that's why the Blue Dot Tour was so successful.

{*twelve*}

AGING AND DEATH

MY DARLINGS,

I hope this isn't too depressing, but I think it is important to talk to you about my getting older and dying.

When Severn was about three, Nana found her stomping on ants and then looking up to ask, "Dead?" As she grappled with the notion of death, she turned to her mom and asked, "Am I going to die too?" It was that horrible moment every parent dreads, when a child first becomes aware of her own mortality. When Nana answered, "Yes, darling, we will all die, but that's way ahead in the future," Severn wailed inconsolably. We wished we could have carried that painful burden for her.

Self-awareness—the recognition of our individuality and our separateness from our mother—is the great blessing and curse of our species. Although we revel in who we are, the awareness that our individual existence is fleeting and that we will disappear forever has haunted humanity since the dawn of consciousness. Why are we here when it is so soon over? Where did we come from, and where do we go? These are the big questions. Did we each emerge simply because our atoms were in the proper configuration? Are we each just a lump of matter that springs to life because it is organized properly, or is there something more? I'm afraid these are questions I'm not qualified to answer.

Throughout time, humans have struggled with the terror and mystery of death and have carried out incredible acts to try to live at least in memory beyond death. Human lives have been sacrificed; great monuments, such as the pyramids, constructed; works of art, music, and literature created; and religions formed—all to provide a comforting sense that something greater cares for us and may enable us to live past our mortal lives. As you know, I am an atheist. I have not studied religion extensively or been tempted by religion's promises, the most ludicrous of which is martyrs being awarded seventy-two virgins in a paradise after death. And, really, eternity is a helluva long time; seventy-two will not go very far. Is virginity even one of the great sought-after goals to die for? Actually, when I was young, making love for eternity might have had some appeal, but now I think it would pale pretty quickly.

When the great Haida artist Bill Reid died, people gathered around to remember him, and someone said, "Oh, Bill is looking down on us and will be so happy listening to us."

Your nana's reaction was "If Bill really is out there, he'll have the whole universe to explore, and I doubt whether he'd be very interested in what we are saying about him."

I don't mean to be disrespectful of religions; most provide excellent guidelines for human behaviour, and I applaud that. But the incredible tales that are spun to pull people in have to be looked at with some humour and perspective. Life—all life, not just ours—is a miracle. I wrote an entire book about one tree to illustrate how miraculous that one life is. Some people feel diminished to think that we are simply expressions of DNA's determination to perpetuate itself, but I am blown away by the thought. Death is a critical part of DNA's search for immortality, because without death, there can be no change, no evolution, and evolution is necessary to adapt to the constantly changing conditions of Earth. Life has flourished through tremendous geophysical change because it has been able to change and adapt to new conditions. It has been resilient because of enormous biological diversity, which allows those best suited to new conditions to thrive over time. Without death to provide space for other, better-adapted forms to take over, life would have been locked into a losing condition. This applies both within and between species. Extinction—the disappearance of species over time—is as critical for life to evolve as death, and 99.9999 percent of all species since life began are extinct.

But knowing the role that death and extinction play in life's survival over the ages doesn't offer me much comfort for my own insignificant and short-lived existence. I find it a miracle that you and I have each come into existence and have grown up knowing joy and pain and happiness and grief and hope and fear and excitement. It's been amazing. I have never dwelled upon the process of dying, though I have watched many loved ones die. Not many ways of dying are pleasant to think about. I suppose one might hope for a very quick death, a painless dying, but I don't think about it much except to know that we're all going to go through it and that it will be a very lonely trip.

What I find impossible to grasp is infinity—endless time and space. I get freaked out at the thought of how totally insignificant Earth is in the cosmos. And when I think of how long the universe—our sun, our planet, and life on it—existed before we were each born, of how brief our existence will be, and then of the immensity of not being anywhere forever after, well, I break off thinking about it or I end up screaming with sadness that David Suzuki, this thinking entity, will vanish, leaving no trace except the atoms that made up my body, forever and ever. It doesn't get any sadder than that.

If accident or infectious disease doesn't kill us, dying usually involves three interlinked parts: aging, dying proper, and death. Aging is not a disease, however, that can be conquered by drugs, better living, or genetic engineering. It isn't a defect.

The minute we define something as a "defect" or a "breakdown of systems," it's the great conceit of "experts" that they can defeat it. The war metaphor serves such experts well, but it is tragic because it is a battle against our own nature.

I have heard doctors refer to the "disease of aging," so immediately one's impulse is to demand that it be cured.

A similar attitude can be seen in the medical treatment of very short people. There is a class of extremely short people called dwarfs, whose stature reflects the lack of or abnormally low levels of a hormone called human growth hormone, or HGH. This condition had been treated with HGH extracted from the pituitary glands of cadavers, and as you can imagine, HGH in this form has been in limited supply and is very expensive. Biotechnology has enabled the production of HGH by microorganisms, however, and the molecule can be harvested in such huge quantities that much more HGH is available than there are dwarfs to treat. As a result, HGH has been marketed to athletes, who use it to enhance their performance, even though it is unknown how effective HGH is or what it does. In addition, a new class of potential recipients has been identified: completely normal people who happen to be on the short end of a normal distribution curve. These people are now labelled as having *idiopathic* (meaning the cause is unknown) *short stature,* a name that sounds like a scientifically validated defect, and *voilà,* there is a whole new group of people to treat with the drug. Just as short people within the range of normal height are considered to have a defect, so aging is looked on as a disease to be treated.

Let me reiterate: Aging is not a disease or a defect. It is a normal process, and to be frank, thank god for aging. If I were just as vigorous as I was thirty or forty years ago, the thought of death would have been far more horrifying than it is now, when I'm feeling the impact of aging. I am grateful that advances have been made in the treatment of organs that tend to break down as one ages—Great-Granddad Harry was treated for heart disease for over thirty years and had a very good quality of life, and kidney transplants have been a big success, too—but the final impact of a gradual diminishing of function of parts of the body cannot be stopped by such heroic intervention.

What is considered old and even what looks old can vary according to culture and conditions. I was fifty-two years old in 1988 when I was filming in the Amazon and met Paulinho Paiakan, a chief of the Kaiapo people who was leading a fight against the proposal to build a dam at Altamira that would have flooded Kaiapo land. He introduced me to his father, who was older than I was but still had black hair. After he told me how old he was, I asked him how old he thought I was. He looked at me with my grey hair and replied in Kaiapo, "Seventy?" I was stunned until I learned that white hair is rare in his tribe, so it is assumed that anyone with white or greying hair must be really old.

When Nana and Severn went hiking in the Annapurna circuit in Nepal in 2003, they met the father of one of their guides and were stunned to learn he was only in his forties. Life in Nepal is difficult, and to live more than forty years qualifies a person as an elder there. It's the same in many First Nations communities, where poverty, alcohol abuse, diabetes, and racism exact a heavy toll, and where average life expectancy can be twenty years less than in the rest of society. There are elders who may be in their forties and who look old.

Like every other aspect of our lives, aging has a genetic component—so yes, long-lived fruit flies or vinegar worms can be selected out and bred so that their offspring will have long lives. Some people have lineages that suggest genes may be partly responsible for long lives. One or two genes may be directly involved in early-onset dementia, certain cancers, and heart diseases, and biotechnology may have a role to play in preventing those diseases. But those who think that longevity may be increased by genetic engineering should remember that for most people, the last years of a long life are often plagued by health and social problems. Surely the challenge is not to prolong a poor quality of life but to improve the quality of those last years.

When I was in my teens, I thought anyone over thirty was really old, and I saw that perspective perpetuated by your parents when they were teenagers. Now that I am an old man, I think, "Gee, that sixty-five-year-old looks pretty good," while I know that you, my grandchildren, think, "Wow, look at that old person!" It's all in your perspective. I still think I'm a relatively young man, but when I look in the mirror in the morning, I am shocked at the old face looking back at me. When I look at pictures of some of the celebrities you all know very well and remark, "Hey, she's gorgeous," it's the echoes of memories and feelings from my young man's brain that respond. And you react with, "Grandpa, that's disgusting!"

I am appalled at the time, expertise, and money spent trying to help people who are aging "stay young." Do not think that cosmetic surgery can somehow miraculously stave off the aging process; it deals with the most trivial part of aging, our external appearance, and I am dumbfounded that so much of medicine is now devoted not to the treatment of illness or life-threatening problems, but to physical appearance. In a time when so many people around the world do not have access to even the most minimal medical care, it is disgusting to think of the money made and skills wasted on cosmetic surgery.

Acceptance of aging is part of getting older; some call it wisdom. And when we accept what we are, then we define ourselves and no longer care how others see us. Believe me, that is totally liberating and gives power to an elder who is speaking.

Your grandmothers, Joane and Tara, were beautiful young women, and it was a tremendous privilege to win their approval and spend a part of my life with each of them as their husband. Today, they would not be called beautiful in the way that women in their twenties and thirties are, but to me, they radiate a beauty. When I look at them, I don't see them in that sexually charged (and therefore totally distorted) way I did when I was a young man. When I was a teenager and testosterone was high, almost any woman looked attractive. Today I look at Joane and Tara through the lens of our shared experiences, and that's what their beauty is to me. To see them as a stranger might, I have to shake my head and deliberately think, "If I were meeting them for the first time, how would they look?" It's the same with your mothers, my daughters. When I see them, I think they are beautiful, and they always will be because they are the sum of memories from their birth onward, and how can that be anything but beautiful?

I still haven't broached the question of how we deal with death itself. When I was a boy, death was more familiar. In my childhood, diseases like leukemia, smallpox, and polio were feared. You have lived through a time when those big killers have been greatly controlled by drugs and vaccines, while the real problems of malnutrition and poverty are not as obvious in Canada as in poorer countries. Now death is something far less familiar for most of us. The first dead person I saw was when we were living in camps in the Slocan Valley during World War II. I must have been about seven or eight. It was summer and I was walking to the beach to go swimming in Slocan Lake when I heard a woman shrieking, "Takebo! Takebo!" in a terrible way I had never heard before. She was running toward the beach, so I followed her. There on the sand was the body of a boy covered in a blanket, surrounded by a crowd. It was the woman's son. I squeezed past people's legs to get a glimpse. All I could see was the blanket and a wet leg protruding from under it. I did not feel sadness or horror that he had drowned but rather was curious to see a dead person for the first time. What made the biggest impression was the sight of a grasshopper that had jumped onto the boy's wet leg. Somehow it seemed so incongruous that an insect would intrude in that moment.

The most difficult situation to handle is when young people die. And on reservations we have seen so many people die far too young. There is an epidemic of premature death among First Nations, whether through car accidents, diabetes, heart attack, or suicide. To me, the suicides are most horrifying. If someone in their thirties or forties doesn't or can't take care of themselves properly and dies of alcoholism or of heart attack through obesity, we resign ourselves to that early death. But when kids in their teens and early twenties deliberately die by their own hands, that is scandalous. Youth are the future. They have to have hope and the feeling that they have everything to live for. And yes, it is scandalous to see the murders of so many indigenous women, whose deaths are ignored, covered up, or rationalized as their own fault; there should be a Royal Commission of Inquiry to investigate them. But suicide is another matter. I cannot bear the thought of the desperation of youth who deliberately take their own lives out of a sense of hopelessness so profound that they have no reason to go on and prefer to die. All of us should be outraged that dealing with First Nations suicides is not one of the highest priorities of our government and our society.

One of the most painful deaths I've experienced was when Shivaji—Ashish and Kajul Duttagupta's child—was hit by a car. Nana and I had met Ashish, a young *Drosophila* (fruit-fly) geneticist at the University of Calcutta, when we were travelling the world in 1972. I had contacted *Drosophila* geneticists in each country we were passing through, asking if it was possible to visit the lab and give a talk on my own work. Ashish was one of the ones who took me up on it, and Nana and I were both absolutely smitten with him.

Ashish and I were the same age, and he had grown up in the part of Bengal that became West Pakistan after partition in 1947. As Hindus, his family had to leave there to move to what would become the province of Bengal in India, and as the lines of Muslims and Hindus passed each other, violence broke out between them and thousands were slaughtered on both sides. Ashish told me he witnessed so many killings and helped cremate so many bodies that he was sick at heart. He used to tell me that the good news was that more than half his life was over.

Because of all the hatred and suffering he had witnessed, Ashish did not want to bring a child into such a world, but Kajul suffered terribly, because in India not having a child is an awful fate for a woman. She would come home every day in tears because of the taunting she received as a childless woman and begged Ashish to relent. So he did, and they had one child, Shivaji, or Ronnie, as they called him. And what a boy he was. You know, if you ask primary-school teachers about special kids, often they will describe someone who is bright, gets along so well with everybody, and is helpful in every way. Those kids come along once in a generation, and they stand out. Shivaji was one of them.

Twice I was able to get funding for Ashish to come and work in my lab for a year. Each time, the people in the lab adored him, because he was so interested in everything going on, so helpful and cooperative, so open and guileless.

Ashish and his family stayed in a basement apartment of my parents' house, and he called my parents Mommy and Daddy. My parents in turn loved Ashish and Kajul and adored their son. Shivaji was very popular with students and teachers and loved school. Every day, Kajul would walk with Shivaji to the school, but one day, he was standing on her right, waiting for cars to go by, when he suddenly darted out into the street. A car coming from the left struck him. I think he was killed instantly, but paramedics started his heart and rushed him to hospital.

I was way up in northern Alberta in a community called Slave Lake, judging a science fair, when Nana called to say Shivaji had been hit by a car. I rushed back to Vancouver as quickly as plane connections could get me there, and when I arrived, I had never seen anyone in such a distraught state as Ashish was. I had thought that coming from a teeming nation where death was such a familiar part of modern history, Ashish and Kajul might be better able to deal with death. But Ashish was absolutely devastated. He called me his guru, and when I walked in, he dropped to his knees, held my hands, and looked up at me with a face contorted with grief and despair and begged, "Guru, please give me one reason why I should go on living. All that ever mattered to me is gone." And I couldn't give him an answer, because he *had* lost the most precious thing in the world to him. I was there when a doctor turned off the machine that was pumping air into Shivaji's body, and it took an agonizing eternity before his heart finally stopped beating.

Ashish insisted on observing the ritual of washing and wrapping his son's body before cremation. I cannot imagine how terrible that must have been for him. At the cremato- rium, we had to hold him up, and when the casket arrived and was put on rollers, he collapsed in grief. Kajul grieved silently. Some said she shouldn't keep it in, but I know she felt that Shivaji's death was her fault, and it tormented her.

I have visited Ashish and Kajul in Calcutta, and they came back to Vancouver once to visit the places where Shivaji played and was hit. They have set up a scholarship at the school in his name, but they have never recovered from the loss. Years later, I was able to give Ashish a reason for living after Shivaji's death. He had become an ardent campaigner to stop the corruption in university that rewarded children of wealthy people; I told him that when he lost Shivaji, death held no fear for him, and that gave him the power to wade so fearlessly into battles with the university. I doubt that this gave him much comfort, however.

I was present when both of my parents and Nana's dad died. Actually, I was in Toronto filming *The Nature of Things* when Tara called to say Mom had suffered a massive heart attack, her heart had been started again, and she was in the hospital. I remember saying to the staff at the show, "I think my mother has died." When I got home to Vancouver, my sisters were there at the hospital, and we all stayed in the room with Mom until she stopped breathing six days later.

Mom had been suffering from dementia for years, though she never failed to recognize us, could conduct a coherent conversation, and still enjoyed life. She had had a meal with Dad, then had gone to a movie, and was walking arm in arm with him when she simply dropped dead of a heart attack. As Dad said, "She had a good death." The problem was that when the ambulance pulled up, the paramedics were obligated to administer resuscitation immediately. They didn't know that Mom had dementia or that her heart had stopped for close to ten minutes or that she would be in a vegetative state if she were revived. So they got her heart going and took her to the hospital, where she never regained consciousness. But my sisters and Dad and I were able to spend that week in hospital both mourning and celebrating that unassuming, hardworking woman who had spent her life taking care of us. She was a good woman, and she had been rewarded with a good death.

Dad mourned her loss for about a year by drinking to excess. But he pulled out of it, I think as much out of love for Severn and Sarika, whom he adored and lavished with attention every day. He lived for ten years after Mom died and found new love with Fumiko Gondo, an immigrant from Japan of Korean ancestry. They met through a shared experience of arthritis. Dad's death was a shock to Fumiko, because she had thought he was so strong that she could keep him alive with food she brought him. I think that when she died a few years later, it was partly from a broken heart. He had treated her so well.

As you know, Dad was my great teacher and mentor. In 1994 he was dying, so I moved in to care for him the last month of his life. And it was a joyous time. He wasn't in pain, he wasn't afraid of death, and he kept saying, "David, I die a rich man," which was puzzling because he had little money and Tara and I were subsidizing him.

Over the weeks I cared for him, we laughed and cried, we talked and talked, but he never once mentioned a closetful of fancy clothes, a big car, or the house he owned in London, Ontario—that's just stuff. We talked about what mattered most to him, and it was all about family, friends, neighbours, and the things we did together. That was my father's wealth, and in those, he was truly a rich man.

When any of us is on our deathbed and reflects on the things that make us proud and happy, I am sure it will not be power or stuff, money or fame; it will be about people and the kind of world and values we leave behind. I hope that at the end of my life, I will be like Dad—in no pain, with no fear of death, and with a mind that is still active. I want you all to be there, not so you can grieve for me, but so I can tell you I did the best I could for your future. I'm just one person, and I couldn't expect to save the future, but I'm like the hummingbird in the South American indigenous story, the one who carried a drop of water in its beak to put on a forest fire. He did this over and over even though all the other animals laughed at him and said it wouldn't make any difference. He kept trying because, as he said, "I'm doing the best I can." I love you all. You have made my life so worthwhile. Thank you.

{*thirteen*}

TAMO

DEAR TAMO, MY FIRST GRANDCHILD,

I am so proud that you recently participated in the protest against the Kinder Morgan pipeline in British Columbia. You did what I would have done myself were it not a risk to my position as host of *The Nature of Things*. After you were arrested (and later cleared of all charges) for civil disobedience, your mom asked me to write a letter of support to a judge. It was never used, but here is the gist of what I wrote:

The world is on a collision course with the things that keep us alive and healthy—the air, water, soil, and variety of life. Corporations, especially those with head offices in some other part of the country or the world, care little for the interests of local ecosystems or communities except insofar as they interfere with the drive to maximize profit for shareholders. They have no obligation to protect local ecosystems

186

or communities. Their sole goal is to make as much money as they can get away with.

You are fighting for the world that will be left to your generation in the future. I believe that what Kinder Morgan and companies like it are doing is what your aunt Severn calls an "intergenerational crime," but there are no legal precedents to pursue criminal charges on that basis.

Before corporations had become so powerful, every generation aspired to leave a better future to their children. That is not on the corporate agenda. There are few legal avenues to protest what I believe is the criminal activity of corporations like Kinder Morgan, so citizens like you are being forced to participate in civil disobedience.

You are taking an active role in the struggle for human rights, social justice, and environmental protection. And you have done this without attempting to ride on or hide under my coattails. You are a role model for young people today.

That is some of what I wrote on your behalf.

When you were born, Auntie Sarika was still a child and Auntie Severn was a young teenager, so you had heavy competition to get me to pay attention, but you have done that. You have used your skills in social media and snowboarding to attract kids to your website, Beyond Boarding, with videos of your boarding stunts, and then you give them information about environmental issues. And through your adventures in Costa Rica and South America you have shown that it's fun and rewarding to help other people and creatures. When you tackled the problems of the Northern Gateway pipeline and the tar sands, you took young people on a fun adventure—travelling in your vegetable-oil-burning bus, hiking up mountains covered with virgin snow, and meeting fascinating characters along the way. Watching the film you made of this adventure, I could see why young people would get hooked. And you ended up in Tahltan country—the Sacred Headwaters—where you learned so much by living with the blockaders and helping to get their story out on social media.

How wonderful that your mom and dad—Tamiko and Eduardo—were avid outdoorspeople and instilled in you a love of nature. They even took you winter camping, something I never did when your mom was a child.

When I was a teenager back in the 1950s, dating a white girl was still a scary thing. Japanese people had been vilified as perpetrators of a "sneak attack" on Pearl Harbor in 1941, and all through World War II, they were portrayed as slant-eyed, bucktoothed fanatics prepared to die for the emperor. I thought I looked just like the caricatures in the posters and grew up feeling self-conscious about my small eyes. Although I yearned to, I never dated a white girl in high school; even in college, I scanned the freshman books for Asian girls at the all-women Smith and Mount Holyoke colleges each year.

I am astonished and gratified that race is not the barrier to dating it once was. Your father, a Chilean Canadian, gave us a greater interest in what was going on in South America, and today I believe it is countries on that continent—Chile, Ecuador, Bolivia, Uruguay, Venezuela, and Cuba—where significant change is happening. Ecuador and Bolivia have actually enshrined Pachamama (Mother Earth) in their constitutions!

What bike fiends your parents were—especially your dad, who got your mom to join him in cycling all the way from Alaska down to Vancouver and then from San Diego up to British Columbia. No wonder you are such an incredible athlete. I didn't know of your father's dream to bicycle from Chile to Vancouver and am sorry he wasn't able to realize that dream. Shifting to a motorcycle to make the trip was still a wonderful idea, and I am sure he had a fantastic time making his way north on his bike. His death in a hit-and-run was devastating, but I hope you find some comfort in knowing that he was living his dream and that he died instantly and so didn't suffer.

Your mom's memorial event for your dad in West Vancouver's Lighthouse Park was a wonderful gathering to remember him in one of his favourite places. When your mom passed out handfuls of his ashes to put somewhere in the park, I scrambled down the rocks to a big tidal pool and threw my handful into it. Immediately sculpins rose and fed on the ashes, and I ran back to tell people that your dad had re-entered the great cycle of life.

Tamo, you have been a remarkable athlete in hockey, football, and especially snowboarding. I know that much of your drive has come from your incredible competitiveness. When I took you to the Seaweed camp of the Gitga'at people from Hartley Bay, you were still a boy, but you were so competitive that you beat everyone else at cards. To this day, they still talk about "that kid who kept winning at cards." That competitiveness is evident now when you play board games up at the cabin.

But I have been filled with the most pride and admiration for your evolution into an activist and for the way you have communicated with other young people. On your trip to the Alberta tar sands, I believe, you were radicalized and became more savvy about getting your message out. It's been amazing to watch how you have used social media to express your admiration and passion for the Tahltans and their struggle to protect the Sacred Headwaters and thus to ignite public interest in their cause.

I was honoured that you asked me for advice and paid attention to my suggestion to meet First Nations people with respect and to spend time listening to them. Now they love and trust you, which is a huge tribute to you. Respect, not guilt or pity, is the key to understanding. I have no idea where you will end up making your mark, Tamo, but you are launched and I am confident that whatever you do, you will do well and with integrity.

fourteen

MIDORI

MY DARLING ONLY GRANDDAUGHTER,

Your older brother, Tamo, has set a high bar for you, and I am sure it helps that you don't have to compete with him as a kid brother might. You are such a beautiful illustration of heterosis, the phenomenon in genetics in which hybrids of two different strains of plants or animals result in vigorous and lovely combinations (I made up the "lovely" part, but I believe that is what happens in humans, and you are lovely). In the early part of the twentieth century, geneticists believed that since different races evolved in different environments, the offspring of interracial couples would suffer "disharmonious combinations," meaning that they would be physically inferior to their parents. But "inferior" is a value judgment, not a scientifically meaningful category. This idea was just another racist assumption in the guise of science that was undermined by the discovery of heterosis.

Having an accomplished older sibling is always a burden for a younger brother or sister, as Uncle Troy, Auntie Sarika, or Cousin Tiisaan can attest. But you have carved out your own persona, your own likes and dislikes, while also supporting your brother in things like his activism. Watching you play soccer and hockey has given me such joy, especially when I think of how much the world has changed for girls since my childhood. As you know, I have three sisters, but my dad's attitude was that girls should finish high school and then get a job... until they find a partner and get married. Can you believe it? That was a very common attitude in the 1950s.

Once, in a high school civics class, the teacher asked what our parents did. I was the only one whose mother worked, and I was embarrassed because we were so poor that my mother had to work. She worked throughout my childhood and teenage years. When she went to high school, she learned to be a secretary, but before the war she washed clothes and sewed with Dad in their laundry and dry-cleaning shop. After the war, she took jobs on farms picking berries and harvesting potatoes, tomatoes, and other vegetables. Then she got a job as a secretary for a construction company. When she and Dad "retired" to move back to Vancouver, she worked in my lab taking care of my fly stocks.

When I was in high school, during the early 1950s, women were expected to raise the family and care for the household while men worked and brought in the family income. A working mother was a sign of poverty. As the women's rights movement began to grow, demanding equal opportunity and equal pay for equal work, enormous opportunities opened up for women. It was a struggle, but now girls can aspire to hope and dream beyond being the roles of wife and mother. Once, math and physics were considered men's areas, but women are making a mark in these fields. More than half of all students in undergraduate and graduate schools, medicine, and law are women, and in traditionally male fields like engineering, agriculture, and forestry, enrolment of women is rising rapidly. This is a seismic shift, and although there remain barriers to many top positions in business and professions, they are bound to be broken by the sheer numbers and talents of women working in those areas.

You may find it hard to believe, but Nana was once rejected for citizenship because she wanted to keep her last name when we married. Nana was born in England and immigrated with her parents to Canada when she was five. But she didn't bother to take out Canadian citizenship until we were married and were planning a four-month trip around the world. She needed a passport and realized she had to take out citizenship in order to get one. This should have been a simple step, but when she applied, she was rejected (her brother, Uncle Pieter, was with her and got his citizenship right away). Nana and I were shocked and outraged. I called the news desk at the *Vancouver Sun* suggesting it would be a good story. The man on the other end of the phone couldn't see why this was of interest. "My wife took my name and loves it," he snorted.

Nana appealed for reconsideration and was called to Ottawa to make her case. She was finally granted citizenship and a Canadian passport, and today a woman's keeping her last name after marriage is no big deal. A few months after Tara got her passport, a woman in the United States encountered a similar rejection for keeping her maiden name, and that was reported in the *Vancouver Sun*.

Today, my darling, I don't sense that you feel any limits imposed by gender on what you choose to do in your life. Your mother and grandmothers were feminists who demanded an end to the sexism that limited their futures. For many women, raising a family is still a priority, but economic conditions may force women to work simply to make ends meet, and we are still evolving ways to support a woman's career opportunities while also raising children.

I am also so happy to see the enormous shift in sexual mores of your generation. When I was young, boys expected to marry girls who were virgins, though there was a lot of hanky-panky going on. After all, teen years are a time of discovery and exploration, and boys are hammered by testosterone. But it meant that girls might use pregnancy to coerce boys into marriage (called "shotgun weddings"), unwanted pregnancies could lead to horrific mutilation or death from backroom abortions, or girls would be sent away to avoid the shame of having the baby, who was given up for adoption. So many futures were truncated by an accidental pregnancy.

Hmm, a letter like this enables me to raise issues I haven't spoken to you about in person. In my youth, contraceptives were difficult or embarrassing to obtain. They were always locked in a cabinet behind a counter, so you had to ask for them, which was excruciating, especially if a pharmacist asked for your age. It was the birth control pill that really launched women on a new path. Women could now control their own fertility, and that has changed everything. Today sex can be explored without fear of pregnancy, and women can call the shots about whom to have sex with without having to make a permanent commitment or limit their own career paths. This has been a radical change in society, and there are all kinds of unintended consequences. For example, fertility declines with age, so women who wait too long to start a family may have trouble conceiving and thus require fertility induction or even *in vitro* fertilization.

Do you remember Seaweed camp? I was so happy to be able to take you there! You got to sit in the copilot's seat and fly into Hartley Bay on a floatplane. Wasn't that exciting? And when we got to the camp, you were happy to bunk with everybody, in the cabin that belonged to Chief Johnny Clifton.

You got on so well with Shelby, and now you are both grown-up, but back then you got to be children, and with her you learned to gather seaweed and prepare halibut and salmon for drying. You experienced the way people have lived for thousands of years. I hope that that experience will remain with you always, because in a city we have such a distant relationship with food and food gathering, and we need to be reminded what food is and how it is harvested.

I believe that diversity is a great strength in society, because the more perspectives one gets on an issue, the better decisions will be. Men and women are different—physically, physiologically, and psychologically—and we should celebrate those differences. It is absurd that half of the population, women, should not have the opportunity to make an equal contribution to society. Women's full participation in society leads to greater gender, ethnic, professional, and economic diversity in all aspects of our world. You are not the only beneficiary of feminism; all of society benefits.

I so look forward to the path you will follow in the future. We've already enjoyed your athleticism in hockey and soccer, and as you make a decision about a career, the opportunities are so great, darling, and Nana and I are rooting for you all the way.

{fifteen}

JONATHAN

MY BEAUTIFUL, BEAUTIFUL BOY,

What joy your arrival brought your parents and grandparents! But the human brain is a complex, oxygen-demanding organ, and it can be damaged, as yours was, when oxygen fails to reach it for even a few minutes during the trauma of birth. The discovery that you have cerebral palsy was devastating, and the diagnosis elicited all kinds of emotions in your parents, I'm sure—guilt at the thought that they had failed in some way, sadness that your future would be so circumscribed by your handicap, and determination to ensure that you would have the most opportunities and the best life experience you could.

I have been amazed and inspired by your parents, Laura and Peter, who have showered you with unstinting love and focused their efforts on maximizing your use of your body and your mind. I am happy that our society gives support—though inadequate and often too bureaucratic—to disadvantaged young people like you. Wheelchairs and teachers trained to deal with special needs have been so important for you as you've grown up. When I was a boy, families felt humiliated if a child was born with a disability and would often hide such a child away.

Every parent wants their children to be physically and mentally healthy. The genetic lottery ensures a wide array of human potential, but during pregnancy and birth there is always the possibility of accidents and abnormalities. I fear that as birthrates drop and parents invest much more time and energy in their children, they demand near perfection. But what is normal? Where is the cutoff for what is acceptable or desirable?

In their drive for perfection, people are now using techniques to try to ensure that embryos conceived *in vitro* do not carry genes that would create a defect. There are techniques to take cells from a developing fetus in order to detect chromosomal and other abnormalities, the most common being Down syndrome, or trisomy 21. This is a slippery slope, especially with Down children, who definitely carry a hereditary defect but whose range of intellectual and physical abilities is quite wide. At what point do we decide that a human being should not exist? I find it a very difficult question.

What if there is a class of fetuses that, at the time of conception, could be predicted to have a high probability of not completing high school; of suffering a variety of problems, including alcoholism, obesity, and diabetes; and of ending up on welfare or in prison? That prediction could be made about those in certain ethnic groups or those who are poor, and clearly racism and discrimination, not biology, are the causes of the prognosis for these fetuses.

Jonathan, you won't remember, but during your early years, your parents read everything they could about the human brain and body and used every means possible to stimulate your muscles and your mind. I was amazed at the way your dad would flip you around, lifting you and stimulating the muscles you needed to balance yourself. Your parents knew that even though you are legally blind, your brain could receive signals from other parts of the visual system, and as a result, you can read. I don't understand how it works, but I know you look at things not directly but at an angle that lets you see from a different part of your retina. The computer and television have been a godsend to you, and you have done so well in school and at home. I am so proud of you.

My darling boy, you have been so brave in confronting the pain of your disability. Do you remember that summer when you came to stay at our cabin on Quadra Island and you caught your first shiner on our dock? How you loved the feeling of speed in our boat as the wind blew through your hair and seaspray hit your face! And you loved the seafood—the prawns and clams and oysters. But because you were going through a growth spurt, the bones in your hips were not articulating properly, so when you were flying back to Vancouver in a small plane and the table dropped down on your leg, it snapped a bone. How excruciating that must have been! You ended up having to get home quickly to Toronto, where complex surgery was performed to get the bones and joint aligned properly.

As your parents have had to adjust their lives to the reality of your special needs and limitations, I have been inspired and filled with admiration. They are ordinary people who have acted with extraordinary strength and love, which is, to me, truly heroic. I believe we define ourselves as a species in the way we treat those who are disabled, handicapped, or in need of special care, and our response affirms that we are an amazing species.

Soon you will be finished with school, and as a man, you will meet new challenges when you consider finding a house that you can share with others. All your life, each challenge for you has also brought great joy as you've met and overcome them. You are my hero, Jonathan, and Nana and I are so proud of you.

{sixteen}

GANHLAANS

DEAREST GANHLAANS,

What happiness you have brought into our lives! Your mother has been an activist all her life and knows the dire environmental path we are on. I asked how she felt about having a child when the world was in such bad shape, and she answered that you were her commitment to continue working to make a better future. Since you arrived on this Earth, you have been a joy who has enriched our lives just by being alive.

Looking back on our lives, it almost seems as if it were predestined that you would come into the world. Nana and I have been deeply involved in Haida Gwaii since the late 1970s, when I first learned there was a battle about logging going on there. I flew to the airport at Sandspit on the islands for the first time in the early 1980s, and I interviewed your *nannai*, Diane, in Skidegate, on the other side of the inlet from Sandspit. Boy, was I scared, because I had heard what a strong person she was. And she was, but we got on well, and a few years later, it was her mother, your great-grandmother Ada, who adopted me.

The film we did for *The Nature of Things* about the battle over logging on Haida Gwaii garnered a huge audience, and letters and phone calls supporting the Haida poured in. The way the Haida stood up to the forest company and the government to fight for the protection of their land inspired people all across Canada. At the time, I didn't think the Haida had a chance against all the forces aligned against them. But Guujaaw, Miles Richardson, and all the elders who are now gone stood together and put their bodies on the line on Lyell Island. They were arrested, but their act prevented logging and eventually resulted in the creation of Gwaii Hanaas, a national park reserve. It was a huge achievement that inspired a nation. Ever since, Nana and I have loved to visit, and when we meet friends there they tell us, "Welcome home." We feel Haida Gwaii is our second home, and now that you and Tiisaan live there, we have all the more incentive to visit often.

The Haida connection to the land has inspired me and also taught me about our relationship with Mother Earth. It was Guujaaw who explained that without that connection, we are rootless and become like everyone else. And Miles has taught me about what it means to be political in the defence of one's land. I never dreamed that the Haida would gain total control over the future of the entire island chain, but that's what they have achieved by holding firm to their claim to all of it.

Your *nannai* recognized something in your mother, and she said she wanted Severn to come to Haida Gwaii for the summer to learn how to live on the land. When she was young, Sev was too shy to go, but as a teenager, she went there and learned so much from your *nannai* about the traditional ways of food gathering and preparation. I remember when Nana and I were going out fishing with Miles and we met your mother with your *nannai* and *chinnai* and Chief Watson Price. Your mother was so happy as she showed us all the salmon she had helped catch and the urchins and scallops she harvested. What a fantastic summer she had! Back then, your father was a full-grown man who was already chasing women. I am sure your *nannai* never thought your mom and dad would get together and marry one day, but she was pretty happy when they did.

What a marvellous place to grow up! You live in paradise. Your mom and dad are very careful to keep you from watching too much television and make sure that you are outside a lot. That is wonderful, and I love visiting and having you show Nana and me around. You already know so much about the place you live in, and you are so observant. I laughed when your *nannai* told me how she took you and Tiis clam digging on the beach below the Ḵay Centre. When she called you over to see a starfish, you took a look and said, "That's a pycnopodia. They are the fastest-moving starfish."

Your *nannai* was flabbergasted. "How did he know that?" she asked me. You are soaking up so many things. I love carrying you on my shoulders so that you can pick salmonberries or thimbleberries off the highest branches. But I don't know how much longer I'll be able to do that as I grow older and you grow bigger. And huckleberries! Mmm, aren't they the best in pies?

A man from Tumbler Ridge, in northern BC, gave me a cast of a fossilized dinosaur footprint found in the town. I was delighted to be able to give it to you because, like Cousin Tamo when he was a boy, you have developed a great interest in dinosaurs. "What do you think it is?" I asked, and you nonchalantly replied, "That must be a theropod footprint." I was dumbstruck because that was exactly what was written on the label but you couldn't read. "How did you know?" I sputtered. "Because it has three toes." At least you didn't add, "anybody knows that!"

Do you remember the night when the tide was low and we went digging clams? It was pretty muddy, and when I turned the light on you, your face and mouth were smeared with mud because you had your head right in the bucket playing with the clams. And when you and Tiis go out to catch prawns, your mom tells me, you both eat them raw as soon as they are in the bucket.

Thank you so much for asking for a treehouse in the woods behind your new home. When I was a teenager, I worked in construction, building houses, and I still love to hammer things together. Over the years, I have built treehouses for your mom and Auntie Sarika, in the dogwood tree on our lot in Vancouver and in balsam trees on Quadra Island, where they spent many happy hours playing. I hope you enjoy the one I built with a lot of help from your dad.

Wasn't that great last summer when we went to the west coast of Haida Gwaii, when the pink salmon were gathered in Bonanza Bay waiting for rain to swell the rivers so they could move up and spawn? They jammed the water, and everywhere we looked, there would be six or seven fish jumping in the air. Each time we cast out our fishing lines from shore, we would hook a fish, and so you caught your first salmon on a hook. Of course, every year you go to Copper Bay, where sockeye salmon are taken in nets and the whole family cuts them up to smoke and bottle. In your dad's boat, you go fishing for halibut and spring salmon and set nets for those wonderful big Haida Gwaii crabs. I can't wait to go up so that you can take me on your adventures. Yet when you visit us in Vancouver, you still want me to take you fishing for shiners! I'm so sorry we don't have great places to fish like you do in Haida Gwaii.

You remind me so much of your auntie Sarika when she was a girl. She had so much patience and would spend hours on the seashore or in the woods just looking, and you are the same. I've watched you in a tidal pool with a dip net in hand, leaning over with your face close to the water—just looking. Suddenly, you dip the net and bring it up to see whether you caught a sculpin or a baby flounder. When we went to the creek by the public playground in Skidegate, I couldn't believe how much time you spent trying to catch minnows, and then succeeding.

I hope you remember our trip to Mo'orea in Polynesia, though you were only four at the time. You told us the plants growing in the place we were staying were only the "hair," that they communicate with each other underground. Nana and I were stunned. Where did you get that idea? And now, before Christmas, your mom says you commented that you couldn't see how Santa could come since reindeer can't fly. And you worried about how Santa could deliver presents when your house doesn't have a chimney.

You are also learning about community. You've already been to pole raisings and feasts, and you celebrated receiving your first button blanket. It was so nice that your kindergarten class made personal cards for elders in the seniors' home and then you got to deliver them to the people in person. That is what community is all about.

You are a thoughtful boy, and I know that more and more I will have to answer "I don't know" to your many questions. But it will be fun trying to find the answer together. I get so much pleasure in watching your world expand before a very curious mind. Thank you for including me in your life.

{*seventeen*}

TIISAAN

HELLO MY SWEET TIISAAN,

Like Midori, you have an older brother to live up to, but you are a joy and delight in your own right. How wonderful it was when you came into this world with a full head of curly hair! And how I regret that when it was cut short, it never grew back with the curls again.

You will, I'm sure, have seen many pictures of you when you were still a baby, wearing what looked like a football helmet with the top cut off. That's because as a baby you would lie on one side all the time, so a flatness developed on that side of your head. You always had a big head of hair, which covered any flatness, but your parents worried that if the flat part got bigger, it might cause a distortion in your face. So they took you to a specialist who fit you with a helmet that gently pushed against your head bones and moulded your head back into a round shape. You ended up wearing that contraption on your head twenty-two hours a day—yet you never complained. I think everyone was astonished at how good-natured you were, accepting that imposition with such aplomb. Of course, you also used that helmet as a battering ram to bang on the wall or hit your brother. You have always been so happy and are such a joy to us. And the helmet worked. Oh, you have a little flat spot, but then so do I, and mine is bigger.

You and your brother are such stunners, and I try to imagine you together when you are older and just knocking people out with your good looks. And you've got those unusual blue eyes, because as you know, Asians and Haida have brown eyes, and it's genes from Europe that result in blue ones. The combination of Haida, Japanese, and English genes has produced a wonderful result! But just because you are good-looking and people ogle you, don't let it go to your head and start thinking you're hot stuff.

The acquisition of language is a fascinating process to watch. Your brother is quite proficient, and although you understand both English and Haida, you haven't yet come out with the proficiency with words that your brother has. I can see that you understand us completely and have a clear idea of what you want to say, but a lot is still Tiisaan language. But I know you will become as fluent as your brother, and I can't wait to hear you jabbering in Haida.

The challenge for you will be to carve out your own interests and desires. You have always wanted to copy whatever

Ganhlaans does. I hated one of the earliest words you began to use: "mine." I can't tell you how many fights I had to inter- 209 vene in because you were clinging to a toy or a bit of wood or even a piece of junk and yelling "mine." Of course, Ganhi always wanted something simply because you had it first. I kept trying to inculcate the notions of "ours" and "share," which I hope will kick in at some point.

You have always responded very strongly to music, especially music with a good beat. You get up and start dancing to Haida drumming and you love to beat the drum, so I have great hopes that you will learn traditional drumming and dancing, which is so important to Haida culture. Ganhi is quite shy in public, but you are a real show-off. I know you will take the lead at feasts and celebrations.

You and your brother are so loved by your parents, your grandparents, and your Haida community, and you are fortunate to be growing up in the confidence of that love and support. There will be times when you are sad, lonely, or upset, when you will be able to draw on that love.

My dear, sweet Tiisaan, how Nana and I wish we could shield you and your brother, Ganhlaans, from hurt that will come during your lives. I've emphasized the love that you are enveloped in from family because that is your shield, your armour against ignorance and bigotry. It pains me to tell you that despite the enormous increase in appreciation of and respect for First Nations in Canada, there is still a great deal of prejudice that will be directed at you. Some people resent what they feel is undeserved support from their tax dollars on reserves, in paying less taxation, in unwarranted claims to land, and so on. Others point to alcoholism, disproportion-ate numbers in prison, or welfare costs without regard to the historical and social causes of many of these problems and as if the accusations apply to all First Nations people.

Your family will buffer you against the pain of any encounters you will have with people who are ignorant and don't know what they are talking about. Know that you are a fine human being who has the love and support of the people who matter. Much of bigotry is based on sheer ignorance. Because we look different from Caucasians (a difference that has a genetic basis), people make a leap to assuming that differences in ability, intelligence, and behaviour are simi-larly determined by genes. That's why, when Canada went to war with Japan in 1942, many Canadians feared people like me and my parents because we looked like the enemy—we were Japanese.

The first time I went to Japan, in 1969, I suddenly felt as if I'd disappeared when I looked at the reflections in a window on the street. Everyone around looked just like me and I had a hard time finding me in the crowd. That's when I realized a lot of my sense of identity was based on looking different in a white society. We may look alike, but the minute I have a conversation with a Japanese person from Japan, a yawning gulf opens up between us because my history is Canadian and British, my music is Beethoven and Gordon Lightfoot, my literature is Shakespeare and Margaret Atwood. That's why some of us refer to ourselves as "bananas"—we're yellow on the outside but white inside.

Your mother had a friend she'd known from primary through high school. Years later, after getting married, your parents met her at a party. At some point, everyone was sitting around chatting and this friend casually mentioned "lazy Indians who are always drunk," but then realized your father is Haida. She tried vainly to apologize to Jud for what she had said, but the words had slipped easily and thoughtlessly from her mouth and illustrated both insensitivity and prejudice. You will have such experiences, but don't let them in any way shake your sense of self-worth.

But Tiis, you are so fortunate in having such a strong supportive family, and that gives you a responsibility to look out for others who might not be so lucky. Bigots who make judgments of others on the basis of religious, ethnic, or gender differences must be confronted. People may no longer express prejudice against you or other indigenous people but focus instead on Muslims or transgendered people—those bigots must be exposed for what they are because they can turn on you in a second.

Whatever you ultimately decide to do, do it with the gusto I've seen in you as a boy. Go for it, and don't worry about whether you'll succeed. Just do it to the best of your ability.

{*eighteen*}

RYO

MY PRECIOUS NEWEST GRANDCHILD,

Your mother was born while I was filming the biggest series I've ever done, *A Planet for the Taking.* Three crews were filming in different parts of the world, and I would fly from one to the other to do my "stand-ups" on location. We had slotted in a three-week period when I could be home with Nana for the birth, but during that period the due date came and went without any sign of a baby. As the days rolled by, I began to get desperate calls from India, from Africa, from Europe: "Where the hell are you? We're getting ready to shoot your stand-ups." Sarika was born weeks late, so I only got to hold her for a day and a half before I left for India. I met up with Nana and your mother several weeks later in England.

In 2014, the year you were born, I was taking another big trip called the Blue Dot Tour, a seven-week bus trip from Newfoundland to Vancouver to get Canadians to support enshrining the right to a healthy environment in our constitution. The date you were scheduled to be born was October 1 (incidentally, your mother's PhD thesis was due by September 30, which was cutting things a bit tight). I left for Newfoundland on September 20, so we knew that unless you came ten days late, I wouldn't be there for your birth. In fact, I was in Saint John, New Brunswick, in the east, when your mother went into labour, and I kept calling throughout the evening to see how things were going. As I talked to Nana, I could hear your mother groaning in the background.

You finally arrived, a big boy, healthy in every way, but I didn't get to see or hold you in my arms until ten days later, when I flew back west for two and a half days just to meet you. I apologized to your mother for my absence during your birth, but she said, "The Blue Dot Tour is about my son's future, so it's okay." And she was right.

Your parents are deeply concerned about the state of the world and your future. As you know, your father has learned about his indigenous background in the last few years. His father, your other grandfather, died all too young before your parents were married. He was a Métis, a person of mixed indigenous and European blood. He was a lawyer and played a big role in getting the return of Kwakwaka'wakw regalia and artifacts from museums in other countries back to Alert Bay, just off of Vancouver Island. In appreciation, he was honoured by being given a very powerful name. When Sarika and Chris were married, a large group of people from Alert

214

Bay came to the wedding and passed Chris's father's name on to Chris. It's a huge honour and responsibility for Chris, and I know you will become part of the Alert Bay community, because he wants to keep close ties with them. That gives me great comfort, because like your cousins, Ganhi and Tiis, those cultural ties with First Nations will shape your relationship with nature and the planet.

As a professional rafting and kayaking guide, your father is acutely aware of how lucky we are to live in British Columbia. He will regale you with wonderful stories of his encounters with grizzly bears, wolves, moose, and so many other animals in the wild. I know he will take you on trips as soon as you are old enough. But Chris also knows that these wilderness areas are threatened by climate change, which is melting the glaciers at an alarming rate, as well as by clearcut logging, roads, and mining.

Your mother has always loved the ocean. As a child, she would always be the first to discover or observe things. She loved to find the smallest creatures—crabs, sculpins, starfish—and like your cousin Ganhlaans, she had incredible persistence, wading into pools or wandering beaches and forest trails for hours, just looking and collecting. She was the first in the family to find porcelain crabs, flat animals under tidal rocks that often had one bigger claw and long antennae. She knew where to go to find salamanders and had the patience to find and catch beautiful nudibranchs. And she is the most patient and successful fisher of all of us.

Ryo

So your parents are great role models. You will grow up loving the outdoors as you learn to kayak and canoe with your dad and as you accompany your mom on field trips for her work in marine biology. They are both avid campers too, so you will learn to love the ocean and rivers and lakes and to care about their perilous state. And because you and your cousins love nature, I know you will become warriors fighting to protect the things you love.

I also know you will grow up with Ganhlaans and Tiisaan, two wonderful cousins. Oh man, the three of you as teenagers walking down a street—what a powerful image! I know you'll visit them in Haida Gwaii often, because Nana and I have a little suite built next to their house, and we will be up there often. I hope you will sleep over in the treehouse I built for Ganhi and Tiis in the forest beside their house. And you will have fights with them, because that's what happens with people you love. But if someone picks on one of the three of you, the other two will be there to stick up for him.

I know you will grow up on the water—your father wanted to name you after a river but had a difficult time choosing a name he liked. After a month without giving you a name, your mom said, "Chris, make up your mind—I like Ryo." Your name is the Spanish word for river (though in Spanish it is spelled "rio"), and they gave you Chilko as a second name, after the great river in the BC interior. A bonus is that in Japanese, Ryo means "dragon," a powerful metaphor to inspire you. What a beautiful name! But it sure took your parents a long time to choose it.

Ryo, I promise you, as I have promised all your cousins, that I will try as hard as I can to work for your future. I'm just one person, but I'm your bompa and will do everything I can to live up to what you expect of me. When I reach the end of my life, I hope I will be able to hug you and look you in the eye as I tell you, "I did the best I could."

nineteen

FINAL WORDS

MY BEAUTIFUL, PRECIOUS GRANDCHILDREN,

In these letters, I have tried to tell you something about my history, my experiences, and my thinking that may help you understand your grandpa a little better—what has motivated me and what I have tried to do in my life. I hope you know I've never tried to interfere with your lives or dictate anything to you. I have such great faith in your parents, whom I love and respect as your role models. In the end, I think we all provide guidance by the way we live, not by words or lectures.

Perhaps, then, the best guide to defining who we are, what we represent, what values we hold is our track record over time. As Severn said in her speech at Rio in 1992, quoting me, "You are what you do, not what you say." Although these are words, I hope these letters will provide a track record of my ideas and actions. But I would like to end with some advice or suggestions that you might consider in your lives.

218   The difficulty I have is in trying to imagine what the world will be like during the rest of your lives. Throughout human history, we could base our entire lives and cultures on nature's cycles and regularities. Indigenous peoples of North America flourished because of the seasonal cycles that governed when plants appeared and animals migrated. After European settlement, the sudden loss of the biomass of passenger pigeons, buffalo, and salmon at the hands of the newcomers had catastrophic consequences for ecosystems—which became less resilient, less productive, and less diverse—as well as for the human societies that depended on them.

Catastrophic events such as earthquakes, floods, droughts, hurricanes, and fires were rare. But that has changed. When so-called once-in-a-hundred-years events like floods or extreme storms begin to occur every ten years or less, something is not right. The human imprint can now be found even on earthquakes and volcanoes. Our species has become a force of nature that is the major factor altering the physical, chemical, and biological properties of the planet. We can't do anything to avoid events that are caused by natural forces, but if *we* have become the major causal factor, we can change our behaviour and activity to reduce the risks and consequences of what we do. That is, in a way, very good news. The difficulty we face lies in the reluctance to make those changes our highest priority.

We have so altered nature that much of what we could do when times were tough in the past is no longer an option. Even in the 1940s, when my family was incarcerated during the war, we could catch fish, gather edible plants and mushrooms, and cut down firewood, though we had to do so surreptitiously because these activities were prohibited. After the war, when we moved to Ontario in a state of poverty, I remember Mom bottling fish Dad and I caught, collecting fruit left on the ground in orchards, and gathering asparagus, blueberries, nettles, and dandelions along railroad tracks or beside ditches. Today, it's harder to find such edible plants or animals, and the ubiquitous spread of toxic chemicals and pesticides means there are health risks even when they are wild.

I think one of the most obscene descriptions of goods today is the word *disposable.* Instead of bragging about durability, resistance to wear and tear, or lasting a lifetime, ads boast of disposability as a convenience, as a sales feature of even big-ticket items such as cars and houses, which can be discarded for bigger, more modern or ostentatious indicators of wealth. We should cover our ears when someone uses the word *disposable* and admonish them for saying a bad word.

When our species came into existence, the planet was already fully occupied and fully developed, but we, an invasive species, have thought of occupation and development in new lands solely in human terms and don't even recognize that our development depends on the productivity and abundance of nature.

220

One way we become blind to what is happening in the world is the way our words are often used to ignore, cover up, or deceive. When we buy seafood, we may have a vague notion that the shrimp we eat were caught along with "bycatch." Often a kilo of shrimp may have been netted along with five times as much bycatch—fish that have too little or no commercial value and so are discarded, even though they are edible and are vital parts of ecosystems. To the fishers, they are just a "waste" of time, effort, and wear and tear. At one time, red snapper, a long-lived fish species that is a prized delicacy to Japanese people, was declared bycatch for fishers seeking halibut, which are bigger and therefore more lucrative than red snapper. Art Sterritt, a Tsimshian friend, told me that one day along the BC coast, he encountered miles of red snapper carcasses discarded by boats fishing for halibut because they were bycatch and couldn't be kept.

Ancient forests that took millennia to evolve are called "decadent" or "overmature," so clearing them is justified by the notion that they are finished or at an end. Sometimes the forest industry labels such forests "wild," and what is planted and grown after it has been clear-cut is called a "normal" forest. We define things in terms of human utility, not in any way that makes ecological or even biological sense.

Trees for which there is no commercial value are referred to as "weeds" that interfere with commercial harvesting. That's what alders were called until a method to make high-grade paper from them was developed, but you'd never know that alders play an important ecological role. They are the first trees to grow after an opening is cleared in a forest, and they fix nitrogen from the air to fertilize the soil for the later-growing, longer-lived, bigger tree species. Yew trees have tough wood with gnarled branches and were called weeds and burned until a powerful anti-cancer agent was found in their bark.

Insects are the most numerous, diverse, and ecologically important (and to me, fascinating) group of animals in the world and only a tiny fraction cause problems for human health or agriculture. It is true that diseases like malaria are transmitted by mosquitoes and in the Arctic, mosquitoes and blackflies are so abundant that they are a scourge for mammals like caribou and humans. But it is their very seasonal abundance that enables millions of birds to migrate, nest, and reproduce there year after year. Yes, they are pests to us, but they are critical components of arctic ecosystems. If we call insects "pests," then we can make war on them. And we have done that, developing powerful chemicals that kill all insects to eliminate the ones that are troublesome to us. To me, using broad-spectrum pesticides is like dealing with high rates of crime in a town or neighbourhood by removing or killing everyone in the area.

There's a battle going on in Canada right now about the use of a new, powerful class of nerve gases called neonicotinoids, or neonics. They kill the target pest insects, but a "collateral damage" is honeybees that are extremely sensitive to the neonics. Even though neonics are banned by the European Union for that very reason, in Canada, commercial interests in this class of pesticides are used to justify their continued use.

222   My most important piece of advice to all of you is to be thoughtful about the way you live. At a time when the global economy dominates our lives, it is easy to buy something without thinking about the global repercussions of that purchase. For example, gold and diamond jewellery comes with a heavy ecological footprint because mining is just not sustainable and some methods of mining are extremely destructive. Shark fin soup is used as a traditional dish for Chinese weddings, but we have become aware of the enormous cost of killing these important predators to get the fins. But do we think about the unsustainability of Chilean sea bass (alias Patagonian toothfish), orange roughy, or bluefin tuna? And think of all the materials that go into electronic products we buy and discard so readily—where do they come from, and where do they go when we are done with them?

I was once on a talk show that was urging people to be more environmentally responsible in the way we live. In the green room, where guests wait before going on the show, a table offered plastic bottles of water brought all the way from Fiji! The program's host was quite embarrassed when I suggested this was a contradiction to what they were trying to do. We've got used to buying and using things without much thought about the true costs. And each time we buy such a product, we encourage its continued production. Before buying anything, you might ask, "Is this sustainable?"

One aspect of being thoughtful to me means thinking

"holistically," that is, considering the context within which the item we're going to buy fits.

We think nothing of ordering a pizza to be delivered, but do we really need it? Is it brought by someone in a car? What kind of car? How far did it come? And think of the box that carried the pizza, the printing on it, and the wax paper inside. What were all these elements they were made from, and are they biodegradable or recyclable? And then there is the pizza itself. If it contains meat, remember that huge amounts of water and energy are required to feed and transport the animals. Were they raised organically? And think of the components of the pizza—flour, sugar, salt, pepper, chili, and much more. Where did each one come from, were they grown organically, how much were workers paid, and were the plants grown in soil that was once covered in forest? I think you get what I mean about being thoughtful about sustainability. It's very complicated in a global economy.

You can see that the repercussions of purchasing even simple goods like clothing, food, and drinks are immense, and when it comes to big-ticket items like a car, computer, or television set, or even a house, the ecological, social, and economic ramifications become enormous. This global system is simply too destructive to be truly sustainable.

Please also think about the way we live at home. Where does the electricity that powers our house, the water that flows through our taps, or even the air that we breathe come from? When we flush the toilet, what happens to the poo, paper, pee, plastic tampon holders, tampons, and condoms that are routinely put into the toilet? What happens to the contents of our blue boxes or garbage cans when they are picked up and put in dump trucks? Everyone should be aware of the source and the destination of these things in our homes.

Canada is a northern country with a limited growing season, yet we can buy fresh fruit and vegetables year round, even in the far north. How is that possible? Canada has more fresh water per capita than any other nation on Earth, yet we seem to accept that there are more than a thousand "boil water alerts" in communities every day. We don't object to paying more for water in plastic bottles than we do for gasoline. We pay even more to buy water shipped from Fiji, Italy, or France. The reason we buy this water from distant lands is that it is supposed to be "superior" to ours in some way, but I am sure that in Fiji, Italy, and France, people buy water brought from other parts of the world, sold on the same claim of superiority. I don't know what you think, but to me, this is insane. It's just water.

For almost all of human existence, we were local, tribal animals, encountering perhaps a few hundred other human beings in a lifetime and travelling over distances limited to a few hundred kilometres max. I don't think it's an accident that we feel most comfortable within neighbourhoods—communities comprising, say, a few dozen blocks in which a local flavour or identity can develop, where local merchants are often known to customers by first names, and where local politicians are held more responsible and accountable by the community. In a northern country like Canada, indigenous people flourished long before there were refrigerators or global transportation because they lived within their ecological means, which were completely local. By becoming as locally self-sufficient as possible (the 100-mile diet was developed by J.B. MacKinnon in Vancouver), we become much more resilient and resistant to the vagaries of global market and other economic fluctuations.

In 1989, economist E.F. Schumacher wrote an influential book called *Small Is Beautiful: A Study of Economics as if People Mattered.* The notion that small is beautiful goes against our belief today that more and bigger are better. But why would they be better? Other than flaunting our economic status to others, why do we need more or bigger when we should be thinking about the quality of our lives?

I have an idea for a science-fiction novel based on the world of the future in which humans have become so numerous that they have used up all the space and all the resources on the planet. After applying every possible technological approach to the problem, genetic engineers come up with a brilliant solution: use biotechnology to create people who are half the average size. This would immediately double the amount of resources and space available while creating whole new economic opportunities in rescaling everything from clothing to homes, cars, and refrigerators. This is just one idea about where our technological optimism might lead. But it's satire, not a serious solution.

Being thoughtful about the way you live also means reflecting deeply on what makes us happy. By happiness, I don't mean the kind of personal ecstatic moment when you ski a black diamond run without falling, climb to the peak of a mountain, or seduce someone you are attracted to. That's what we in the West tend to think when we say "happy." In the small, economically poor kingdom of Bhutan, hidden in the Himalayas between India and China, the new king's father declared that the goal of his society was not economic growth or development but happiness.

The Bhutanese are Buddhists, and happiness is seen there as coming from a sense of belonging or having a place in society, of living where nature flourishes and where there is adequate medical care, low infant mortality, and universal education. These are all measurable indicators of happiness. This is quite a departure from Western society, in which economic growth and consumption are seen as the measures of success rather than as a means to a higher goal. As part of its pursuit of happiness, Bhutan protects over 70 percent of its forest cover, is 100 percent organic in its food production, emphasizes the wearing of traditional Bhutanese clothing, and controls tourism, which can be highly disruptive of society. Whether Bhutan will withstand the impact of television and its ads and the allure of economies based on hyperconsumption is still a question. But how refreshing to consider the economy as simply a means to attain a higher goal of happiness!

In Ecuador, under President Rafael Correa, who was trained as an economist in the United States, the constitution was rewritten to enshrine the rights of Pachamama

(Mother Earth). In other words, it's not just people who are guaranteed constitutional protection, but nature itself. This makes a real difference: in a legal suit taken up on behalf of the Vilcabamba River, for example, a judge recognized the river's rights by ordering its restoration after a road-building company dumped rocks, sand, and gravel into it. Like the people of Bhutan, Ecuadorians do not define progress by economic growth. Instead, they set the goal of their country as *bien vivir* or *sumac kawsay,* the Quechua term for the "good life," a notion similar to the happiness of Bhutan.

You know that as Japanese Canadians, my family, like all the First Nations, didn't have many of the rights that Caucasian Canadians enjoyed, especially the right to vote. And during World War II, the rights we did have were abrogated by imposition of the War Measures Act. So now that we have gained rights all others have, I hold those rights in great esteem, especially the right to vote. I believe that democracy is the best system devised so far, but it is still far from perfect, especially the first-past-the-post system in Canada. In each riding, the candidate who gets the most votes wins. If candidates from two or three other parties garner significant support, they can split the votes between them so that someone with only 30 or 35 percent of the votes can win. So most parties, left and right, don't form governments with the support of a majority of voters.

For democracy to function as it should, citizens have more than a right—they have a responsibility to be involved. Active involvement is not some kind of frill or indulgence;

it is a fundamental responsibility, and I hope you will all fulfill that responsibility.

Democracy is only as good as the people participating in it, and we never get enough participation. Once elected, any politician has to think about getting re-elected, and that means doing things that he or she hopes will keep voters' support. Now imagine political candidates appealing for support so that they can implement programs that will cost enormous sums of money that may benefit "future generations." It would be political suicide; yet that is what is needed to confront issues like climate change, toxic pollution, and habitat destruction.

Children and future generations don't vote, so they are not on the agenda. That's why I urge parents and grandparents to be warriors on behalf of children. We have to put their interests and their futures on the political agenda and make politicians serve them as well as us. When there are deliberate attempts to monkey-wrench democracy, as when robocalls are used to misinform certain groups about where their polling stations are, all who believe in democracy should howl with outrage and demand that the perpetrators be punished and pledge not to condone or support such practices.

Another suggestion: slow down. I mean, why are we in such a hurry? We are all going to end up in the same place—dead—and we lose so much in our rush to get through life, to do things, to go somewhere. I have spent a lot of time filming in exotic places like the Amazon, the Arctic, Papua New Guinea, and Australia, yet often the pressure to "get stuff in the can" and move on to the next location means I have no time to take in the places I visit. Sometimes when I am back in Vancouver or Toronto and viewing the rushes, I will think, "Oh yeah, I kind of remember that," and regret that I didn't fully experience the place while I was there.

Being thoughtful about how you live also means being kind and generous to others. I find I derive far more pleasure and satisfaction when I share with others than when I hoard something for myself, because the act of sharing affirms that we are members of a community and that the community matters to us. Even though we as a species have moved from living in rural villages to inhabiting big, crowded cities, we seem more isolated from each other than ever. It used to make me uncomfortable that in Japan, people always speak to you. Whether you get into an elevator or onto an escalator or when you enter a cab, you will be formally greeted or welcomed. But now I treasure those rituals as acknowledgments of my presence. We need rituals like that. Hartley Bay is a remote village of some two hundred people on Canada's west coast. There are no cars there, since all the houses are connected by an elevated wooden boardwalk. So people are constantly walking along the boardwalk, and even though they may pass each other several times per day, they always greet each other with a "hi" or "hello." To me, it's as if each salutation is an affirmation that they know each other is there, and that they are together as a community.

Today we retreat into our homes, which are twice as large as homes were forty years ago and are loaded with electronic entertainment. Even when we walk down the street, we wear earbuds hooked up to electronics or text or talk on our phones, shutting down our other senses, which inform us about the world around us, and shutting out other people. If you have ever taken an elevator for several floors or ridden a bus, you know that everyone avoids eye contact and finds ways to occupy themselves, including talking on a phone. There's something wrong with that. In subways in Japan, there are signs everywhere admonishing people not to talk on cellphones because it interferes with the community of fellow riders.

I know that for all of you this is redundant, but when you find partners, and if you have children, please spend as much time as possible outside, unplugged, so that you can hear, see, and smell the world around you. Why do you need to go outside? For one thing, to appreciate what it is that keeps you alive. And the more time you spend outside, the more you are able to sense change in that world. If you can smell something, chances are that unless it's flowers or food, it doesn't belong there and is not good for us. But even more profound, we have to get outside and seek nature because we need that connection for our physical and mental health.

I hope you can find ways to acknowledge, be grateful for, and celebrate the things that matter most to us. By these things I mean our ultimate mother—Earth—for her generosity in providing all we need to survive and enjoy health and well-being. We have to develop little ways of reminding ourselves how important air, water, photosynthesis, soil, food, and other species are. Just get outside and revel in the sun's warmth on our skin or the snowflakes that tickle our faces, take swims in freshwater rivers or lakes, and watch the rain create puddles for children to play in. These are joyous acknowledgments we can make right through the year, not the orgy of consumerism that overtakes us in December.

Finally, each of you might think about your life, what you hope to do with it, what your goals are, or what your vision of the future might be, and then what you might be proudest of when you become an elder like me. I can tell you, you are my legacy, for which I am most proud and happy. I can't take much credit for who you are and what values you hold, but I do take pride and joy in your mothers and the partners they chose, in whose lives I had a much bigger hand. I hope my love will remain with you throughout your long and happy lives.

With all my love,
Your Grandpa

NOTES

CHAPTER 3

1. Victor Lebow, "Price competition in 1955," *Journal of Retailing* (Spring 1955).
2. Pablo Ruiz Nápoles, "Consumption, economic theory and the American way of life," *Voices of Mexico*, vol. 69 (2004): 30–33.
3. Frank Pellegrini, "The Bush speech: How to rally a nation," *Time*, September 21, 2001.
4. John Maynard Keynes, "National self-sufficiency," *The Yale Review*, vol. 22, no. 4 (June 1933): 755–769.

CHAPTER 9

1. Will Steffen et al., "Planetary boundaries: Guiding human development on a changing planet," *Science*, January 15, 2015.
2. Terry Erwin, "Tropical forests: Their richness in Coleoptera and other arthropod species," *Coleopterists Bulletin*, 36 (1983): 74–75.

3. A.D. Chapman, *Number of living species in Australia and the world,* 2nd ed. (Canberra: Australian Biological Resources, 2009).

4. Christine Del'Amore, "Species extinction happening 1000 times faster because of humans?" *National Geographic,* May 29, 2014.

5. George Monbiot, "It's time to shout stop on this war on the living world," *The Guardian,* October 1, 2014, at http://www.theguardian.com/environment/georgemonbiot/2014/oct/01/george-monbiot-war-on-the-living-world-wildlife.

CHAPTER 11

1. The paper is available online at www.thebreakthrough.org/images/Death_of_Environmentalism.pdf.

2. Carl Sagan, *Pale blue dot: A vision of the human future in space* (New York: Random House, 1994).

3. David Boyd, *The right to a healthy environment: Revitalizing Canada's constitution* (Vancouver: University of British Columbia Press, 2012).

OTHER BOOKS BY DAVID SUZUKI

The Sacred Balance:
Rediscovering Our Place in Nature, Updated and Expanded
ISBN 978-1-55365-166-6

The Legacy: An Elder's Vision for Our Sustainable Future
ISBN 978-1-55365-828-3

Everything Under the Sun: Toward a Brighter Future on a Small Blue Planet
(with Ian Hanington)
ISBN 978-1-55365-528-2

Tree: A Life Story
(with Wayne Grady, illustrated by Robert Bateman)
ISBN 978-1-55365-126-0

David Suzuki: The Autobiography
ISBN 978-1-55365-281-6

More Good News: Real Solutions to the Global Eco-Crisis
ISBN 978-1-55365-475-9

You Are the Earth: Know Your World So You Can Help Make It Better
ISBN 978-1-55365-476-6

Visit www.davidsuzukibooks.com for exclusive content,
a digital download of this letter, and information about David Suzuki's
extensive list of books, including new and upcoming titles.

DAVID SUZUKI FOUNDATION

The David Suzuki Foundation works through science and education to protect the diversity of nature and our quality of life, now and for the future.

Our vision is that within a generation, Canadians act on the understanding that we are all interconnected and interdependent with nature. We collaborate with scientists, communities, businesses, academia, government, and non-governmental organizations to find solutions for living within the limits of nature.

The Foundation's work is made possible by individual donors across Canada and around the world. We invite you to join us.

For more information, please contact us:

The David Suzuki Foundation
219–2211 West 4th Avenue
Vancouver, BC, Canada, V6K 4S2
www.davidsuzuki.org
contact@davidsuzuki.org
Tel: 1-800-453-1533

Cheques can be made payable to the David Suzuki Foundation. All donations are tax-deductible.
Canadian charitable registration: (BN) 12775 6716 RR0001
U.S. charitable registration: #94-3204049